The Turn
of the
Screw

Bewildered Vision

TWAYNE'S MASTERWORK STUDIES
Robert Lecker, General Editor

The Turn
of the
Screw

Bewildered Vision

Terry Heller

TWAYNE PUBLISHERS • BOSTON
A Division of G. K. Hall & Co.

The Turn of the Screw: Bewildered Vision
Twayne's Masterwork Studies No. 26

Copyright 1989 by G. K. Hall & Co.
All rights reserved.
Published by Twayne Publishers
A Division of G. K. Hall & Co.
70 Lincoln Street
Boston, Massachusetts   02111

Copyediting supervised by Barbara Sutton
Book production by Patricia D'Agostino

Typeset in 10/14 Sabon with Goudy Handtooled display type
by Compset Inc. of Beverly, Massachusetts

Printed on permanent/durable acid-free paper
and bound in the United States of America

Library of Congress Cataloging-in-Publication Data

Heller, Terry, 1947-
    The turn of the screw : bewildered vision / Terry Heller.
        p.   cm. — (Twayne's masterwork studies ; no. 26)
    Bibliography: p.
    Includes index.
    ISBN 0-8057-8080-7 (alk. paper).   ISBN 0-8057-8123-4 (pbk.)
    1. James, Henry, 1843-1916. Turn of the screw.   I. Title.
II. Series.
PS2116.T83H38   1989
813'.4—dc19   88-7583
                                                                            CIP

Contents

Note on References
and Acknowledgments

For this study I have used the text of the New York Edition of James's works as reproduced in the Norton Critical Edition, edited by Robert Kimbrough (1966). Two kinds of page citations to this volume appear in my text. References to the text of *The Turn of the Screw* appear as page numbers alone in parentheses. References to secondary materials in the Norton Critical Edition appear as page numbers following "NCE."

I extend my thanks to: Coe College for released time and the use of a computer and software; Randy Roeder and the Stewart Memorial Library of Coe College for invaluable assistance in obtaining illustrations and other materials; the Houghton Library of Harvard University for access to and permission to reprint the photograph of Henry James in front of the Palazzo Borghese, Rome, 1899; the New York State Historical Association Library for access to and copies of the illustrations that accompanied the original publication of *The Turn of the Screw* from *Collier's Weekly*; the Coe College Department of English and other faculty as well for support and help; the University of Illinois Press for permissions to accept the contract for this book and to develop ideas from *The Delights of Terror* (1987) in this study; *Gothic* for permission to reprint portions of "Perspective and the Implied Reader in James's *The Turn of the Screw*," in chapter 2 (the article was forthcoming at the time of this book's composition); Barbara Sutton and the staff of Twayne Publishers for essential help in completing the manuscript; my family, Linda and Gabe, for unfailing help and support; my parents, Rollin and Betty, for giving me a good start. This book is for my parents.

Henry James in front of the Palazzo Borghese, Rome, in 1899
(attributed to Giuseppe Primoli).
Reproduced by permission of the Houghton Library, Harvard University.

Chronology:
Henry James's Life and Works

Although most of James's fiction was published first in magazines—serials for longer works—and later in book form, most of the dates below indicate first book publication. The main exceptions are the ghost stories, which are dated by first magazine publication, and *The Turn of the Screw*, for which each important publication is listed.

1843	Born 15 April, at 2 Washington Place, New York City, second son of Henry James, Sr., (1811–82) and Mary Robertson Walsh (1810–82). James, Sr., was the son of William James (1775–1832), who emigrated from Ireland and made a fortune in real estate. James, Sr., after a religious conversion, became a follower of Emanuel Swedenborg and achieved contemporary fame as a writer on religious and philosophical subjects. Mary Robertson Walsh descended from a prosperous Scots-Irish, New York family. Henry James Jr.'s older brother, William (1842–1910), achieved eminence as a philosopher and psychologist, authoring *The Varieties of Religious Experience* (1902).
1845	Birth of Garth Wilkinson James (d. 1883).
1845–1855	Educated privately by governesses and in day schools in New York City and in Albany.
1846	Birth of Robertson James (d. 1910).
1848	Birth of Alice James, Henry's only sister (d. 1892).
1855	Serialization in *Frank Leslie's New York Journal* (January–June) of *Temptation*, which Leon Edel believes influenced *The Turn of the Screw*.
1855–1860	Travels with family in Europe; attends schools in Switzerland and France.

1860	In part because of the outbreak of the Civil War, family returns to the United States, taking up residence at Newport. Begins friendships with artists such as John LaFarge and William Morris Hunt; studies art with Hunt and reads voraciously; translates Merimée's "Vénus d'Ille," a supernatural tale.
1861	Helping to put out a fire, incurs a lower back injury painful and debilitating enough to prevent his enlisting in the Union army with his two younger brothers.
1862–1863	Begins law at Harvard, but does not complete his studies.
1864	Moves with family to Boston and begins friendships with James Russell Lowell and William Dean Howells. Begins professional writing career with book reviews for the *North American Review*.
1865	First short story, "The Story of a Year," appears in the *Atlantic Monthly*.
1866	Moves with family to Cambridge, Massachusetts.
1868	"The Romance of Certain Old Clothes" and "De Grey: A Romance" (supernatural tales).
1869–1870	Travels alone to Europe, visiting England, France, Switzerland, and Italy. While in England, learns of the death of Minnie Temple, the first woman he seems to have seriously admired.
1871	*Watch and Ward*, first novel, serialized in the *Atlantic Monthly*.
1872–1874	Returns to Europe, traveling widely, living in Paris, Florence, and Rome.
1874–1876	After spending a winter in New York City, resides in Paris, where he meets and cultivates friendships with Ivan Turgenev, Gustave Flaubert, Guy de Maupassant, and Émile Zola, among others.
1874	"The Last of the Valerii" (supernatural tale).
1875	First two books appear: *A Passionate Pilgrim and Other Stories* and *Transatlantic Sketches* (travel essays).
1876	"The Ghostly Rental" (supernatural tale). *Roderick Hudson*, first novel to appear in book form. Moves to London and meets more writers he admires, notably George Eliot and Robert Browning.
1877	*The American* (novel). Visits in Paris and Rome.
1878	*Watch and Ward* (first novel) appears in book form; *French Poets and Novelists* (criticism); *The Europeans* (novel).

1879   Visits in Paris and Italy. *Daisy Miller* (novella); *An International Episode* (novella); *Hawthorne* (critical biography). *The Madonna of the Future and Other Tales.*

1880   *Confidence* (novel). Travels in Italy.

1881   *Washington Square* and *The Portrait of a Lady* (novels). Returns to the United States, mainly because of his mother's failing health.

1882   Mother dies in February at Cambridge. Returns to England and visits in France. Founding of the Society for Psychical Research, the publications of which kept supernatural topics before the reading public for the rest of James's lifetime. His brother William and several of their friends became members and officers of the society. Father dies in December at Cambridge. Returns to the United States to help settle family affairs, before taking up permanent residence in England.

1883   First collected edition of novels and tales in fourteen volumes. *The Siege of London* (tales) and *Portraits of Places* (travel). Death of Garth Wilkinson James.

1884   Visits Paris. *Tales of Three Cities.*

1885   *A Little Tour of France* (travel) and *Stories Revived* (tales in three volumes). Alice comes to England, placing herself intermittently under his care. An invalid, she suffers from depression and "hysteria." (Oscar Cargill argues that *The Turn of the Screw* reflects James's observations of Alice's illness and treatment.)

1886   *The Bostonians* and *The Princess Casamassima* (novels). Leases a flat in Kensington, making his London residence more permanent.

1887   Spends most of year in Italy and Switzerland, often in the company of Constance Fenimore Woolson, his most intimate female friend of this period. Woolson was a novelist and the grandniece of James Fenimore Cooper.

1888   *Partial Portraits* (criticism); *The Aspern Papers* (tales); *The Reverberator* (novel).

1889   *A London Life* (tales).

1890   *The Tragic Muse* (novel). Decides seriously to attempt writing plays.

1891   "Sir Edmund Orme" (supernatural tale). Dramatization of *The American* moderately successful.

1892   "The Private Life," "Sir Dominick Ferrand," and "Owen Wingrave" (supernatural tales). *The Private Life* (tales); *The Wheel of Time* (tales); *The Real Thing and Other Tales; Picture and Text* (art criticism); *Essays in London and Elsewhere* (variety of subjects). Alice James dies of breast cancer in March.

1894   Constance Fenimore Woolson, probably James's closest female friend, dies in Venice, apparently a suicide. *Theatricals* (two unproduced plays).

1895   Enters in his notebook 12 January the "germ" or seed for *The Turn of the Screw:* the previous Thursday (10 January) heard from the Archbishop of Canterbury, while a guest at dinner, a vague story of wicked servants who corrupt orphans left in their care and who, after dying, continue trying to get and hold the children. "The Altar of the Dead" (supernatural tale); *Theatricals: Second Series* (two unproduced plays); *Terminations* (tales). London production of *Guy Domville* is moderately successful; however, a "riot" on opening night in which James is jeered on stage convinces him that he is a failure in the theater.

1896   "The Friends of the Friends" (supernatural tale); *Embarrassments* (tales); *The Other House* (novel). Begins dictating virtually all his fiction to a stenographer.

1897   *The Spoils of Poynton* and *What Maisie Knew* (novels). Writes to his sister-in-law 1 December that he has completed *The Turn of the Screw*; "I *have* at last, finished my little book— that is *a* little book" (NCE 107).

1898   *The Turn of the Screw* (supernatural novella) serialized in *Collier's Weekly* January through April. *The Two Magics*, containing *The Turn of the Screw,* significantly revised, in book form; *In the Cage* (novella).

1899   "The Real Right Thing" (supernatural tale) and *The Awkward Age* (novel). Spends summer in Italy.

1900   "The Great Good Place," "Maud-Evelyn," and "The Third Person" (supernatural tales); *The Soft Side* (tales).

1901   *The Sacred Fount* (supernatural novel).

1902   *The Wings of the Dove* (novel).

1903   "The Beast in the Jungle" (grouped by James with his supernatural tales); *The Ambassadors* (novel); *William Wetmore Story and his Friends* (biography); *The Better Sort* (tales).

1904   *The Golden Bowl* (novel). Visits the United States for the first time since 1883.

Chronology: Henry James's Life and Works

1904–1905	In addition to visiting family, tours the Midwest, South, and West, delivering well-received lectures "The Lesson of Balzac" and "The Question of Our Speech."
1905	*English Hours* (travel).
1906–1909	Revises his fiction, some works extensively, and writes prefaces for the New York Edition of his "collected works." Revisions of *The Turn of the Screw,* though important, are not numerous.
1907	*The American Scene* (travel). Begins writing plays again.
1908	"The Jolly Corner" (supernatural tale); *The High Bid* (drama) produced in Edinburgh and London: *Views and Reviews* (criticism)
1909	*Julia Bride* (novella) and *Italian Hours* (travel). Suffers from nervous disease.
1910	*The Finer Grain* (tales). Travels with William James to Germany where his brother grows more seriously ill with heart disease, while Henry's health improves. In Switzerland, learns of the death of youngest brother, Robertson. William dies soon after Henry accompanies him home in August.
1911	Receives honorary degree from Harvard. Returns to England.
1912	Honorary degree from Oxford University.
1913	*A Small Boy and Others* (autobiography).
1914	*Notes on Novelists with Some Other Notes* (criticism) and *Notes of a Son and Brother* (autobiography). Deeply disturbed by the outbreak of World War I in August, as he had been by the Civil War, The Spanish-American War, and Boer War. Becomes extensively involved in refugee and hospital work.
1915	Becomes a citizen of Great Britain, in part because of war regulations and in part because of love for his adopted home. Suffers a stroke 2 December, beginning his final illness.
1916	Receives the Order of Merit from King George V. Dies in Chelsea 28 February. Ashes are buried in the family cemetery at Cambridge, Massachusetts.
1917	*The Middle Years* (autobiography, unfinished).
1921–1923	*The Novels and Stories of Henry James* (Collected Edition, 35 vol.).

1

The Historical Context

America and Europe

Henry James was a product of Western civilization in the nineteenth century. His intimate understanding of the American mind is probably attributable in part to his family background. He was the son of an independently wealthy, gentleman intellectual. He grew up knowing Ralph Waldo Emerson and the other philosophers and poets of Emerson's circle. On the other hand, he spent significant portions of his youth in Europe as well, and after 1870 he resided there, mainly in England.

By choosing the social, aesthetic, and intellectual life of Europe as most stimulating to his art, James acquired a past and a future. To him America seemed unaware of its past and naive about its future. To some extent he dramatized this attitude in his successful early novella *Daisy Miller* (1879). Daisy, a typical and wealthy American girl, behaves, according to one character, as if she were in the golden age, as if the fall of Adam and Eve had never happened. She seems to live in the blind faith that nothing very bad can ever occur, that her future must be as rosy as her brief past. As a result she neither understands nor takes seriously the kindly advice of her expatriate friends in Rome. Her adventures end in an error of hygiene that could have been prevented had she not been so cut off from "the old world"; she dies from malaria contracted while visiting the Colosseum by moonlight.

In England James found a usable past that seemed missing in America and a view of the future that included multiple moral as well as technical possibilities. The American culture he left behind was on the whole rapt in a dream of technological mastery of the self, the American landscape, and the world. During James's adult life, bounded by the American Civil War and World War I, the United States changed from a rural agrarian into an urban industrial society. Chicago, one extreme example, grew from twenty thousand in 1850 to two million in 1910. This growth also reflects the westward expansion of the population. By World War I the geographical and political union of the United States was complete, heavy industry was the dominant economic force, and the country was beginning to assert power in world affairs. The dominant mood for most of this period was optimistic, though James's contemporaries such as Mark Twain and William Dean Howells were pointing out flaws and weaknesses in this optimism.

The English culture into which James moved comfortably was quite different. Though England also was going through significant changes, there were established traditions that made the past seem real and important. James needed this backdrop against which to understand and represent his great subject, the individual mind in its social relations. Social relations in Europe seemed to James a richer field than in the United States. They led to complex fates, and to characters who considered rather than assumed the future in their decisions. His celebrated "international theme" consists in part of exposing "simpler" Americans to the complexities of European social relations and of bringing complex Europeans into the simplified relations of America.

American and English culture shared a characteristic that was important to James's artistic success. In the latter half of the nineteenth century, it became possible for a hard-working writer to earn a living by his pen even if he did not often produce best-sellers. Among the reasons for this fortunate state of affairs was the appearance and success of great literary magazines such as *Collier's Weekly, Nation,* and *Atlantic Monthly.* James had a good start because he was able to continue a kind of apprenticeship until he was past thirty, depending upon his family's wealth to supplement his income. Once he was on his own in Europe, however, he was able to live adequately, eventually even quite comfortably, on the income from his reviews, travel sketches, and fiction. His residence in England also made it easier for him to publish in both countries simultaneously, thereby overcoming the disadvantages of the lack of an international copyright law.

THE VICTORIAN MIND

Three aspects of social and intellectual life in England are especially relevant to *The Turn of the Screw*: Victorian attitudes toward religion, class, and sex. In *The Victorian Frame of Mind* Walter Houghton characterizes the Victorians as essentially ambivalent on each of these subjects.

Religion. Increasingly, people of all classes found that traditional Christianity had the same intellectual status as the superstitions they denigrated in "primitive" peoples. At the same time they felt that belief was essential to an orderly society. Out of this opposition came a will to believe. It was characteristic of Victorians to assert dogmatically Christian beliefs and the superiority of Christianity over other religions, not out of tranquil faith in its absolute truth, but rather out of fearful doubt of the consequences of giving up belief. Though Houghton connects this trend with many others in the Victorian age, it seems to be at the center of a generally growing uncertainty about all truths that might once have been considered absolute. To overcome this uncertainty, Victorians tended to speak their beliefs more loudly, to will upon their experience the structures they wished to prevail.

The will to believe comes into being to silence doubt, to repress the voice that threatens individual mental order and ultimately social order as well. But that voice cannot be silenced. Doubt cries out for certainty, and Victorians expressed this desire in their interest in fantasy. At the same time that Victorians were accepting that accounts of Christ's miracles were superstition, but affirming the truth of Christianity, they were dabbling increasingly in much less grand, but at least accessible, supernatural manifestations. During James's lifetime, a Society for Psychical Research scientifically investigated hundreds of cases of supposed contact between the dead and the living.

Victorian doubt, therefore, found its heart's desire in Victorian fantasy, not merely in numerous reported meetings with the dead, but also in an explosion of literary fantasy. Among James's contemporaries were such important fantasists as Bram Stoker, Sir Arthur Conan Doyle, Robert Lewis Stevenson, Lewis Carroll, Oscar Wilde, and Algernon Blackwood, to name just a few.

Class. The Victorians were also ambivalent about class. During the nineteenth century the vote was extended to ever larger numbers of people. Restrictions of property and sex gradually disappeared. At the same time "a specter" was "haunting Europe." Socialist revolution was continuously in the air, calling up for English conservatives the worst of the French Revolution. While the equalizing of power among segments of English society made life more comfortable on the whole, there was also great uneasiness, a feeling especially among those who held power and property that the newly enfranchised would wrest away these privileges. At any moment revolution might break out and the social fabric crumble into chaos. The Victorians' response here paralleled their response to religious doubt; they dogmatically asserted the importance of maintaining the system of class distinctions.

Sex. Like religion and class, sex among the Victorians is too complex a topic to treat more than superficially here. Victorians tended for many reasons to be deeply fearful and distrustful of procreative energy. One sign of this fear was the view of woman as "an angel in the house." Religion fueled concern about sexual matters, focusing it on the family.

The Historical Context

According to Houghton, the sexual urges were connected in the Victorian mind with the forces of unbelief and revolution. As Victorians responded to uncertainty and fear of social disorder with a will to believe and a will to order, so they responded to this threat in part with a combination of repression and a religion of love. Sexuality was seen essentially as a degrading animal drive to be rigidly controlled. But, they came to believe, sex was sanctified and transformed within marriage. This was achieved largely by the power of virtuous women, who in their nature and increasingly in their nurture were apart from the fallen world. Kept pure and innocent of the world's ways until marriage, they were to have absolute sway over the moral life of the family. One of the goals of this arrangement was to secure the family from the destructive forces of society: the various social and economic problems that led to tremendous female poverty and prostitution in the society at large, to high divorce rates, and to the growing feeling among social observers that society was in moral decline.

The Turn of the Screw is carefully set in Victorian England. Uneasiness about religion, class, and sex pervades the tale. These tensions prove fertile ground for James's cultivation of the individual mind in its social relations.

2

The Importance of the Work

In *"The Scarlet Letter": A Reading,* Nina Baym ably sets down the main criteria by which a literary work is judged great in modern Western culture: literary skill, originality, traces of an original sensibility, emotional and intellectual impact, and touchstones for our lives.[1] James's novella clearly displays all except perhaps the last of these qualities.

From the first reviewers to the most complex recent readings, nearly all of the many, many persons to write about the novella have testified to its unique power to engage the emotions and the intellect. Nearly a century after its composition, the tale is still generally agreed to be the greatest tale of terror written in English. It is certainly one of the few tales of terror to be elevated from the category of popular literature for mass consumption to high literature, a work we want to pass on to future generations. James's writings about his intentions have convinced critics that he was highly self-conscious in constructing the tale, and also in speaking about it—perhaps rather coyly—after its publication.

Students of American literature would find it difficult to confuse James's voice with any other writer's. Though William Faulkner, for example, could convey the inner mind in similar sentences, he did not examine the kinds of minds James chose for his subjects. James tended to select a consciousness finer than most readers have, yet to make it so clear to the imagination that for a moment the reader seems indeed to possess just such a mind. These minds are capable of exquisite observations of and inferences about other people. Usually, these abilities are in the service of deeply held values that seem, at least, both good and beautiful.

When Baym discusses *The Scarlet Letter,* she points out how characters and situations in that novel have become part of modern consciousness. It is difficult to say the same about *The Turn of the Screw.* The governess, the children, and Mrs. Grose have not yet become archetypal, associated with familiar human experiences. Instead, what has seized the foreground of readers' attention is the problem of interpreting the text. It offers itself at first as entertainment, but problems of interpretation are soon apparent. Indeed, *The Turn of the Screw* has become celebrated in American literature as a text with two mutually contradictory readings. The problem reflects precisely the difficulty the governess, the central character, explains she has with the children. She finds two contradictory ways to understand them; which is correct?

This kind of dilemma is universal in the modern period, as the Victorians were realizing when they tried to deal with the decline of the authority of Christianity. If there is not one absolutely true way to interpret the cosmos and human experience, then a person is in the position of choosing between several provisional ones whenever an important decision is to be made. The governess's position reflects the effects of a growing and disturbing moral pluralism. When modern society has more fully come to terms with the loss of absolutes, James's novel will probably seem more universal than it does now. In that future moment the governess's dilemma may be seen as an archetypal modern experience.

The Turn of the Screw is a great work because it has continued since its publication to give pleasure and to tease us into thought. Like Keats's grecian urn, this tale raises more questions than it answers.

3

Critical Reception

Critical discussion of *The Turn of the Screw* has moved through three major phases since 1898. At first, the tale was read as a literal ghost story, though several reviewers felt there was something more in it. Then, with the advent of psychoanalysis, many critics thought they could discover and articulate that "special something." They began a lively debate over whether the ghosts that appear in the tale were real or hallucinations of the narrator. This controversy was partially resolved in the third phase of critical discussion. To understand how criticism of *The Turn of the Screw* has developed, it is necessary to review the main features of the plot.

The novella has two main parts: a short prologue by an unnamed narrator and an autobiographical narrative by an unnamed governess. The prologue describes events taking place fifty years after the events the governess narrates. Douglas, one of a group gathered for the Christmas holidays at an English country house, reveals that he has a manuscript in which a governess describes the apparition of ghosts to two children. Douglas became friends with his sister's governess during one of his summer vacations from the university. The governess told him this story and eventually gave him her written account. He is persuaded to read it for the assembled company.

Critical Reception

The governess's story concerns her first job. When she is about twenty, she accepts the position of governess to a pair of orphans, ten-year-old Miles and eight-year-old Flora. Their uncle and guardian places upon her the unusual condition that she handle all matters involving the children by herself, without bothering him. Despite initial doubts about taking on so much responsibility, she finds the country house where the children live; the staff, especially Mrs. Grose, the housekeeper; and the children themselves charming, friendly, and helpful. Gradually, she discovers that ghosts seem to be haunting the house and grounds and that these ghosts are interested in the children. Further observation and investigation lead her to the conclusion that these are the ghosts of Miss Jessel, the former governess, and Peter Quint, the uncle's deceased valet. She learns that Mrs. Grose believes the two were lovers and the children were in some undefined ways participants in this illicit relationship.

The governess tries to find ways of protecting the children, but she cannot, for the children seem to desire communication with the ghosts. The governess's position is complicated because she is the only person to admit that she sees the ghosts; therefore, she is never perfectly sure that she does not imagine them. Furthermore, despite much circumstantial and inferential evidence, she is never perfectly sure that the children communicate with the ghosts. She loves Miles and Flora dearly and is unwilling to introduce them to thoughts of evil if she is mistaken in her interpretation of what she has seen.

A crisis occurs, forcing the governess to confront the children or risk losing them to the ghosts. She confronts each separately. Flora denies having seen Jessel's ghost and then becomes feverish. Mrs. Grose takes her to her uncle. Believing Miles willing to confess the secrets behind his unexplained behavior, specifically, his being expelled from school and his having recently taken and destroyed a letter from the governess to his uncle, the governess remains at Bly with him. She believes that if he confesses, he will be free of the ghosts. He does confess, but before completing the confession, while the governess can see Quint's ghost and he cannot, Miles suddenly dies.

From the beginning *The Turn of the Screw* was recognized as one of the great ghost stories. Most reviewers immediately placed it at the peak of the Gothic tradition. Readers justified this response by referring to their feeling that there was something "extra" in *The Turn of the Screw*. In his preface to the New York Edition (1908), James indicated that he had deliberately left unspecified the true intentions of the ghosts. He had provided his readers with a blank to fill with whatever evil they could imagine, and he was delighted with the results (NCE 122–23). He also hinted that the governess's interpretation of her experiences lacked authority (NCE 121). Contemporary reviewers responded strongly to his evocation of vague evil, while later critics took up his hint in a way that made *The Turn of the Screw* one of the great subjects of literary debate.

For early reviewers the focus of horror was the children. Some found the tale too repulsive to recommend because of the suggestions of young children being involved with sexual evil, first with living fornicators and then with their ghosts. Such a story violently subverted Victorian popular psychology's strong presumption of the pristine innocence of children. What might have been the circumstances of the intercourse between ghosts and children? How could children willingly participate in such perversity? How could ghosts be so evil?

In his biography of James, Leon Edel offers evidence that James did not share the popular notion of childhood innocence. James's own childhood had made him painfully aware of the violence children could perform in their imaginations. Other scholars have argued that James's care of his sister, Alice, and of others who suffered from mental disorders had made him deeply aware of the power of the unconscious mind. Partly as a result of the work of his brother, William, Henry was aware of the developing ideas about the unconscious mind in Paris and in Vienna, where Sigmund Freud (1856–1939) was publishing his early studies. The governess, however, fully accepted the doctrine of the innocence of childhood, as did many of the novella's first readers.

In 1934 reading of *The Turn of the Screw* changed radically. In that year Edmund Wilson published a widely read Freudian interpretation of the tale. There were hints of the possibility of change earlier. For example, in 1907 Oliver Elton expressed doubt about whether the governess had saved Miles from the ghosts (NCE 174). In the 1908 preface James dropped his hint that the governess's interpretation of events lacked authority. In about 1920 Harold C. Goddard wrote but did not publish an interpretation in which the governess hallucinates the ghosts and constructs an account of their purposes in an unconscious attempt to satisfy her unacknowledged sexual desire for the children's uncle (NCE 181–209). Virginia Woolf, in a 1921 essay, argued that the central horror of the tale is in its unbroken silence, in what it fails to reveal (NCE 179–80). In a 1923 study of the American short story F. L. Pattee sketched a reading in which the governess was insane and the children her victims (NCE 180). Edna Kenton published in 1924 a discussion that emphasized the degree to which James "protected" the governess, that is, left her free to tell her story without authorial intervention. The result of such protection was the governess's exposure, for she has no authority at all to support her account. Kenton concludes that the governess's narration is an externalized symbolic representation of her inner struggle.[2] Edmund Wilson seized upon Kenton's general idea in his 1934 essay that, because of his reputation and wide readership, forced a change in the way *The Turn of the Screw* is read.[3]

Wilson's argument is essentially the same as Goddard's unpublished argument of 1920. The governess is sexually frustrated. She must avoid awareness of her sexual desire, which was awakened by the uncle. She unconsciously creates the ghosts and their persecution of the children to deal with her frustration. Though Wilson acknowledged that the tale could be read either as a ghost story or as the story of the governess's hallucinations, he insisted that the latter was James's intended meaning. When he revised this essay in 1948, Wilson cited new evidence to justify backing off from the assertion that James intended the governess to hallucinate, though he still believed the tale should be read this way. In 1959 Wilson returned to his original position. Wilson's interpretation was neither elaborate nor very accurate, but it stimulated others to fill it out in detail and with greater plausibility.

With Wilson's essay began the debate that has produced volumes of print many times the length of James's masterpiece. Are the children really haunted by evil ghosts, or are they victims of a neurotic governess who appropriates them to her own psychodrama? This question has been formulated in various ways, but has remained at the center of critical discussion of the novella since 1934.

Perhaps the most important cultural change reflected in this turn of critical opinion was the popularization of Freudian psychoanalysis. Whereas only a few intellectuals and doctors had heard of Freud's work and of other discussions of the unconscious in 1898, nearly any reasonably educated Westerner would have a good deal of information, however superficial, about Freud's ideas in 1934. It is remarkable that after Freud had so effectively cast doubt upon the sexual innocence of children, the focus of interpretation should become the governess's rather than the children's psychology. Freud had described childhood development as an emergence from infantile polymorphous perversion (taking sexual pleasure in all bodily functions) toward an adult centering of sexual pleasure in the genital stimulation that accompanies procreation. His description of the Oedipal and Electra stages of sexual maturation painted a picture of "perverse" curiosity and murderous fantasies behind cherubic faces. Though few who understood Freud would have held out for the natural innocence of children, those who applied Freud to *The Turn of the Screw* invariably chose the governess for case study.

Opposition to psychoanalysis of the governess soon appeared, producing eloquent and careful arguments such as Robert Heilman's in 1948 (NCE 214–28). The effect of the opposition was to place psychoanalysts in their proper position, but not to close debate. Clearly, if on the surface the story is about ghosts, then the burden of proof should fall upon those who find a covert meaning beneath this surface. Defenders of the ghost story turned mainly to close examination of the text, but also to James's comments and to biographical and cultural materials, to produce evidence against which the psychoanalysts had to make their case.

The debate between these two positions continues, but in the early 1980s an important new factor made itself felt. Psychoanalysis had been undergoing critical revision at least since Freud's death in 1939. Jacques Lacan (1901–81), French psychoanalyst and leader in the revision and elaboration of Freudian thought, became an increasingly important influence on literary criticism. Lacan's discussions of the limits of psychoanalysis, though often very difficult to understand, called critics' attention to the peculiar nature of the unconscious. Lacan emphasized that the unconscious mind is inaccessible to the conscious mind in any ordinary way, but especially by means of language. The unconscious expresses itself in symptoms and in what we would normally call failures of language. Hallucinations are symptoms. Slips of the tongue are failures of language. Lacan's work emphasized that the analyst's attempt to interpret such signs amounted to putting into language what language has been unable to communicate. The analyst who overtly interprets a patient's symptoms imposes meaning upon them, perhaps at the expense of the patient. Only the patient can possess the authority to validate an interpretation of the symptoms.

From this point of view, the governess's narration is part of her construction of her self. Part of her problem is that her whole self includes both her conscious identity and the unconscious "Other" that she cannot know by means of language. As James's earliest readers recognized, there is a blank or silence in the governess's narration. While her whole self is revealed, only her conscious self is directly presented in language. The insight offered by Lacan tends to affirm that in a highly self-conscious narration such as hers, the unconscious part of the self will probably be present, but on the other hand, Lacanian thought insists on the silence of this presence. No one except perhaps the governess herself can say with authority what the content of her unconscious is. By protecting the governess in the way Kenton describes and by making evil in the tale a blank in the way James explains in his preface, James has given the governess the freedom to be a fully rounded character with an unconscious to be expressed but not articulated in her narration. One result, as both James and Kenton point out, is that her authority as an interpreter of what she sees is undermined.

Christine Brooke-Rose in 1981 and Shoshana Felman in 1982

published studies of *The Turn of the Screw* and of criticism of the tale that explore the implications of the silence of the governess's unconscious. They argue that previous psychoanalysis of the governess has shown an unjustifiable eagerness to explain what was in her unconscious. In fact, the crucial feature of her unconscious is its silence. As Virginia Woolf said so insightfully in her 1921 review, *The Turn of the Screw* is pervaded by a silence that is never broken. That the governess sees ghosts and interprets them in the way she does may indeed prove that she is undergoing some unconscious events. Furthermore, the oddities of her behavior may hint at what those events are. But there are many ways of reading meaning into these events, and no coherent reading can easily claim precedence over any other. As in successful psychoanalysis, the final authority on the correctness of a "reading" of one's unconscious is oneself, and that authority is equivocal. When one attempts to say unequivocally that the governess hallucinates and to explain precisely why she does so, one is filling a blank, speaking for silence. The meaning found in that silence is the perceiver's meaning. In fact, the meaning is likely to say more about the perceiver (the critic / analyzer) than about the perceived (the governess under analysis).

From the perspective provided by Lacan, the governess exceeds her authority when she undertakes to impose upon the children her reading of their unconsciouses. But even though we can see that she has exceeded her authority, we readers exceed our own if we in turn impose our reading of the governess's unconscious upon her. This perspective alters but does not eliminate the central problem of determining the meaning of this story.

If the ghosts are real and the meaning she reads is correct, the governess saves the children. If there are no ghosts, she harms the children. But even if there are ghosts, if she reads their meaning incorrectly, she still harms the children. The Lacanian perspective forces the reader / critic into the position of not being able to determine whether the governess is correct in perception or in interpretation.

In their interpretations Brooke-Rose and Felman moved toward the position that this tale is absolutely ambiguous. The text says there are ghosts and the text says there are no ghosts, but only a hallucinating narrator. The governess says she saved Miles but reveals she may have destroyed him. There may be no way within the text of escaping these ambiguities. Such a conclusion would lead to seeing *The Turn of the Screw* as an example of what Tzvetan Todorov has labeled the fantastic.

In *The Fantastic* Todorov describes a literary effect that appears in many works but is the central effect of only a few. The reader experiences the fantastic in fiction when he or she hesitates between a natural and a supernatural explanation of the events that take place in what appears to be a natural world.[4] Todorov sees *The Turn of the Screw* as an example of a "pure fantastic" work, in which this hesitation is not resolved toward either a natural (mad governess) or a supernatural (real ghosts) interpretation, but instead is sustained through the end of the text.[5] If Todorov is correct and *The Turn of the Screw* is absolutely ambiguous, then critics must concern themselves with the problem of how to read such a text.

Reading *The Turn of the Screw* becomes like looking at the familiar optical illusion in which a drawing is either two faces in profile or a vase. Under the normal conditions of perception, the human mind will not let the drawing represent both pictures, but instead alternates the meaning of the lines in a persistent and uncomfortable vibration between the two interpretations.

A READING

4

Introduction

Why Is This Reading a <u>Re</u>reading?

At the end of *The Turn of the Screw* a horrifying event takes place, the death of Miles. His governess describes the event in this way: "We were alone with the quiet day, and his little heart, dispossessed, had stopped" (88). After those words, not another appears in the text. The story, however, does not end there. Indeed, it circles back to the beginning in the prologue, where another narrator introduced the governess's account by revealing something of what happened to her after the death of Miles, two aspects of which are of special importance: she continued a successful career as a governess, and she twice told the story of her first job.

One reason the following "reading" of *The Turn of the Screw* is a rereading is that the tale does not end with its last words but rather begins anew. As the critical reception reveals, this story has demanded rereading. On first reading, it seems to present itself as a thriller—a perceptive and heroic governess battles to save innocent and beloved children from evil ghosts. But at the end of that reading, a terrifying question arises. The governess asserts that Miles's little heart is dispossessed when he dies, but how does she know what has happened in the silent heart of the dead boy? She loves Miles, so she wants to believe she has saved him, but neither she nor we readers can be sure she has.

Once this question arises, the whole tale reopens for interpretation. We must reread it to discover whether there is information we missed that will shed light on this question. We feel the need for certainty about what happened to Miles and about the reliability of the governess's judgments.

Circling back to the prologue, with its information about the governess's subsequent career, is provocative but not immediately helpful. It appears that no one has held her responsible for the terrible events at Bly, the country home of Miles and Flora. Upon introducing the story Douglas, to whom she has given the manuscript, gives her the highest recommendation as a governess in his family, where she worked ten years after Miles's death. The only indication of something unusual in her subsequent life is that she tells Douglas her story, first orally during hot summer afternoons on his shady lawn after his second year at Trinity, then again in a carefully written manuscript delivered to him shortly before her death, about thirty years after Miles's death.

Why should she wait ten years to tell her story to anyone? Why then should she tell it to Douglas?

When we look at her relationship with Douglas for answers to these questions, we remember that they liked each other: "I liked her extremely and am glad to this day to think she liked me too. If she had n't she would n't have told me" (2). Remember, now, that we are rereading. Having just read the last chapter in which Miles confesses that he was expelled from school for saying "things" to those he liked, we reread the prologue to discover that the governess has told this tale to Douglas because she liked him. Here is an unexpected connection between Miles and the governess. Both have said "horrible things" to those they liked.

Whatever Miles said was sufficient to have him expelled when those things were repeated to masters and eventually to the headmaster. What the governess said has had its effect too. The narrator of the prologue makes clear that Douglas has found it difficult, yet necessary, to repeat the governess's tale: "He had broken a thickness of ice, the formation of many a winter; had had his reasons for a long silence" (2). Why should this occasion bring out this story after forty years of silence?

Let us digress for a moment to notice the process of rereading we have begun. We began with the last words of the novella because they left us uncertain about whether Miles was saved or damned when he died. Going back to the prologue, we discover another question. Why did she delay telling her story until she met Douglas, ten years after Miles's death? Implicit in that question is another we have not yet raised: Why tell such a potentially embarrassing tale at all? In considering why she told Douglas—because she liked him—we came to yet other questions. The main one so far is what to make of the observation that Miles says horrible things to his friends and the governess tells her horrible tale to her friend. While such questions might be taken up differently by different readers, what is significant in this process is that one is impelled back to the prologue after reading the last chapter. Though we do not find there an immediate answer to our questions about Miles's fate and the governess's judgments, we find promising, newly significant material. James seems deliberately to have planned for a rereading, for the story actively meets the returning reader. This reading is a rereading because the last sentence forces us back to the beginning and, when we return, we discover a new book.

Returning to the question of Douglas's broken silence, we notice that two major factors contribute to his telling the story: one, the story of Griffin's ghost provokes him to break his silence, and, two, the company, especially the narrator, with whom Douglas seems quite intimate, is congenial. Though there is no definitive evidence that the narrator of the prologue is a woman, one critic, Linda Kauffman, has made a case for thinking so. I will speak of the narrator as female, not because I am certain that she is a woman rather than James's own voice, for example, but because doing so helps to keep before us that special bond the narrator and Douglas affirm between themselves. At any rate, Douglas makes a point of considering the narrator, to whom he is quite close, as the main audience of his reading. She is the one who will understand it rightly; to her he eventually gives the governess's manuscript.

Returning from the last chapter to the prologue, we discover a series of repetitions.

1. Miles confesses saying "things" to his friends.
2. Miles dies.
3. Ten years pass.
4. The governess tells her horrible tale to Douglas, whom she likes.
5. Twenty years pass.
6. The governess gives Douglas a copy of her tale.
7. The governess dies.
8. Twenty years pass.
9. Douglas tells the tale to the narrator whom he likes.
10. Time passes.
11. Douglas gives the narrator the governess's manuscript.
12. Douglas dies.
13. The narrator publishes the manuscript.

This list raises even more questions. Miles's confession and death seem to lead to parallel confessions and deaths far into the future. Information like this, resulting from our return to the prologue makes it seem necessary to reread the entire text in the ambiguous light of its end. What the prologue reveals about the governess's experiences after the death of Miles does not create the story's missing epilogue.

The history of the criticism of *The Turn of the Screw* is a history of rereading. To read the many critical pieces on the tale is to observe keen, thoughtful, and somewhat desperate minds grappling with this text, poring over it in great detail, using every intellectual tool and every kind of information that seems at all relevant. All of this rereading results from two crucial features of the story. One is that it is great. Virtually no one has denied the power of *The Turn of the Screw* to grip, hold, and move its readers. The other is that something is not quite right; the tale evades interpretation. There is something about it that needs to be said but has not been, a mystery at its center.

It is this mystery that has led directly to psychoanalytic interpretations that declare the governess an unconscious murderess. This interpretation could arise from any of several points in the story, but its central provocation is Miles's death. This event, as noted, should send the reader back to the prologue for further information about Miles's fate, and it undercuts the governess's account. That account is easily undercut because, as James suggested in his 1908 preface to the New York Edition, he has not given any supporting authority to her interpretation of events at Bly (NCE 121).

Readers who come to the end of the text and who, as a result of Miles's death, decide that the governess is likely to be mistaken in her assertion that Miles is dispossessed, then find themselves able to reconstruct the governess as a flawed perceiver and interpreter. In the history of the reading of *The Turn of the Screw*, this reconstruction has led to psychoanalyzing the governess.

In a widely accepted version of this reading, the governess falls in love with the children's uncle. She is so young and inexperienced that she is unable to deal with this passion consciously, so she represses it, hiding it from her consciousness. This repression is unsuccessful because her unconscious grasps subtle hints in her experience to discover that her predecessor, Miss Jessel, became the lover of Peter Quint, the uncle's valet, when he was temporarily in charge at Bly. Her unconscious makes Quint and Jessel into actors of its desires. Jessel, a lady, gave herself to a man of lower class, much as the governess wants to give herself to a man of higher class. The governess's unconscious creates a symbolic "show" that threatens to make her consciously aware of her secret desires. Because the ghosts mean what she wants to deny about herself, she wishes to banish them.

Just as she projects her unconscious guilt upon the ghosts, she projects her innocence upon the children. She comes to see the ghosts as attacking them. She must protect her own innocent consciousness from knowing what her unconscious sees in the affair of Quint and Jessel. The external events she "witnesses" are really representations of internal events, her own psychological struggle to control sexual desire and achieve mental wholeness. The projection of innocence on the children serves her needs in another way as well, for it allows her to be heroic in public. She may "save" the children in the service of the uncle she loves, perhaps to earn his love, since she cannot have it in the normal course of affairs. In this version of events, her telling the story to Douglas is a continuation of her attempts to earn the love of one above her station by exhibiting her heroics.

While constructing such an interpretation requires rereading, its goal is to end reading. Indeed, the goal of all interpretation, traditionally understood, is to end reading. This is not to say that all critics expect to say the final word about a text's meaning, only that they hope to settle at least for the time being those questions the text seems most insistently to raise for them. All sophisticated readers know that new questions will arise and that old questions thought closed will be reopened as culture changes. *The Turn of the Screw* is special among literary works mainly because it insistently raises for all its readers questions that cannot be settled, with the result that the immediate process of interpreting becomes endless. Rereaders who accept the governess's story at face value are denied the assurance of Miles's salvation they desire. And psychoanalysts who believe they have said the last word on the governess repeatedly encounter the challenges of adherents of the supernatural interpretation.

What these readers want is closure, the sense that the literary work has come to its appropriate end and resting place. The history of the criticism of *The Turn of the Screw* suggests that neither the supernatural nor the psychoanalytic interpretation is ultimately satisfactory. Despite meticulous examinations and refinements of these positions, readers have not been able to agree that either of these closures is the correct one. The result has been virtually continuous rereading during the half-century since Edmund Wilson gave wide publicity to the idea of the governess being neurotic. More recent readers have concluded that the tale is unreadable. By this they mean that *The Turn of the Screw* is truly ambiguous. One can read it completely through as either a tale of ghosts or a tale of neurosis. One cannot rest content with either reading once it is complete, for always one comes to the governess's assertion that, though he is dead, Miles is saved. If we have trusted her account, how do we deal with the lack of proof that he is saved? If we have not trusted it, how do we account for the governess never being held responsible for this crime? She should at least feel guilty.

Though I know of no one who has published an argument that such ambiguity simply makes *The Turn of the Screw* a bad work, I have heard frustrated students voice the beginnings of such a position. While it is important to recognize the special ambiguity of *The Turn of the Screw,* it is not satisfying to do so.

Human beings want works of art to be complete and understandable. We are willing to accept great difficulties and frustrations if they end in a satisfying closure. Most mature minds recognize that the patterns we impose upon experience are provisional and temporary. Nevertheless, the mind depends upon being able to impose categories of order upon experience. Whereas Christianity once revealed to all members of Western civilization who they were, what their relations to each other should be, and what they should do, since about the eighteenth century, people have tended more and more to look to art for ways of ordering experience.

It may be for this reason that we want closure in literary works, and for the same reason, James may have deprived us of that finality. This rereading of *The Turn of the Screw* is intended to explore the ambiguity, the unreadability that demands rereading.

READING AND REREADING

To explain rereading it is helpful to make clear first what I mean by reading. I believe that the meaning of *The Turn of the Screw* occurs in the process of reading it. In this way I identify myself and my method of reading with the reader-response group of critics.

Most of the works of literature that become classics share a quality we call universality. This means in part that they remain fairly easily accessible to readers over centuries. Whether or not the authors intended their work to speak to readers beyond their immediate audiences, these works have, in fact, done so. James wanted very much for his fiction to be universal.

The readers of a novel that remains accessible for centuries will vary in many ways. They will vary over time in the culture they share, as indicated in the changing ways we have read the tale. A novel's readers will also vary at a given time, as can be seen in the continuing controversy over how to read this story.

At its most radical reader-response criticism interests itself in the almost infinite variations of reading experience that distinguish every single individual reader's reading from every other reading. I am more interested, however, in regularities, in what individual readers share with each other when they read the same text. This reading of *The Turn of the Screw* is an attempt to articulate and, inevitably to some extent, to influence a shared reading.

Along with Wolfgang Iser, I see a text as a series of response-inviting structures. The author has laid out these structures in a particular order in an attempt to control, within certain limits, the reader's mental activity for the duration of the text. The author wants not only to hold the reader's attention, but also to convey a particular series of experiences that will eventuate in a kind of wholeness.

The mind is too various and the word too limited and slippery for the author to hope to control absolutely the responses of readers. Otherwise, the greatest works of art might well produce universal agreement about their meaning. As it is, even authors as self-conscious of their art and purposes as James was cannot explain fully what meanings they may have intended by a particular choice, whether as large as a character or turn of the plot or as small as a word or gesture. And, as critics such as Stanley Fish and Norman Holland have shown, what goes through the mind of a reader as he or she reads is shot through with accident and idiosyncrasy.

Nevertheless, we observe in writing about texts considerable agreement between different readers' experiences. This agreement tends to be about the larger features of the text. For example, while it may be frustrating that there are two contradictory interpretations of the governess's character, it may be consoling that only these two are shared widely.

The foundation of this agreement is at least double. On the one hand, there is the author's attempt through the manipulation of language to control the reader's response. The author tries to bring the reader to a conception of the wholeness of the work that approximates the author's own vision of that wholeness. On the other hand, the reader also desires to discover the wholeness that seems embodied in the text. The reader works with the signs of the text to construct provisional wholes, working continuously toward the creation of a final whole that will amount to a satisfying closure. The reader takes up each new piece of data discerned in the text and accommodates that information to his or her sense of what is happening or alters that sense to incorporate the new fact.

We can observe this process in the opening sentence of the governess's narrative: "I remember the whole beginning as a succession of flights and drops, a little see-saw of the right throbs and the wrong" (6). We come to this sentence from the prologue that has told us how the governess came to take this job. Upon first reading, we are unable to tell where her story begins, what the whole beginning is that she is speaking of. These questions point toward the next sentence, which locates us in the chronology of her narrative. We are asked to construct an idea of what she considers to be a beginning.

Also related to chronology is where the governess places herself in time. That she remembers confirms that the narrative was written some significant time after the events to be narrated. Reader and governess are in the time of her writing. We are asked to set aside our real present and to join in her remembering and composing. In doing so we adopt a perspective. This perspective is not immediate presence at the events to be narrated, but a meditative hovering over them. This hovering is accented in the governess's creation of metaphors: flights and drops, see-saws, throbs. Her narration is carefully considered, the words weighed. There is a reaching after the appropriate way of expressing how she felt, rather than the breathless grasping of the handy word that we might expect of someone presently involved in the horrors of seeing ghosts.

This observation leads to another major structure that we begin to build, our evaluation of the governess's character. Her first sentence richly suggests and questions some of her personal qualities. Her memory is that in the beginning her experience seemed to swing between the very good and the very bad. She makes this distinction almost playfully here. She begins a language game with her metaphors of alternation, a game that continues in various forms throughout her narrative, and much of this play seems self-conscious. She suggests here that she is aware of playing language games, that she thinks about her metaphors. This play makes it problematic later in the text to decide whether her plays upon words like *turn* and *revolution* are at all deliberate, and whether her puns on names and allusions to *Hamlet* belong to her or to James.

The governess's first sentence reveals some of the response-inviting structures of *The Turn of the Screw*. Reading that sentence carefully engages one in constructing several wholes, among them the chronology of the narrative, the governess's perspective, and her personality. Reader and text continue to interact in this way until the reading is complete and the reader is satisfied that the significant features of the text fit together. When the experience of the text seems whole, the reader has the satisfaction of aesthetic completion. One of the reasons we read texts through to their ends is to achieve this final aesthetic pleasure of completion. The human mind is such that we delight in creating meaning. Works of art are valuable to us in part because in the nonthreatening circumstances of playful leisure, they exercise our powers of creating meaning.

That the literary text invites us to construct wholes has special implications for reading *The Turn of the Screw*. The unique problem of this tale, which has led to my writing a rereading, is that it seems truly ambiguous. For most readers, it seems to embody two distinct and mutually exclusive wholes. If one reading is true, the other is false; yet, neither reading can submerge or eliminate the other. Rereading is necessary because the book compels it. If, however, the novella is truly ambiguous, there may be no end to rereading. Like the governess on her see-saw, the reader may remain forever alternating between the two main perspectives of interpretation. One purpose of this rereading is to determine whether the text provides any descent from this precarious perch.

Introduction

I have one more aspect of reading to explain before looking more closely at what rereading entails: the implied reader. In *The Act of Reading*, Wolfgang Iser says, "No matter who or what he may be, the real reader is always offered a particular role to play, and it is this role that constitutes the concept of implied reader."[6] The first sentence of the governess's narrative takes the reader out of his or her time. We know that we do not fully lose awareness of whatever time and place we have chosen for reading. Rather, we shift perspective. As we will see in the discussion of the prologue in the next chapter, by the time we arrive at the governess's first sentence, we have moved through several changes in time perspective. In this process we have been constructing provisional wholes of various kinds, already looking toward a sense of the wholeness of the work. By entering into this process, we also begin the construction of provisional selves, the appropriate reader of this work. Iser argues that the response-inviting structures of a literary text constitute a reader fitted to read the text.

Any healthy human mind contains potentially an infinite variety of personalities. Out of this variety we become individual persons or identities. This individuality is called forth and maintained by all the forces of our culture and biology, including, humans continue tending to believe, our own free choice. But even our identities are not fixed. We daily adjust the self we present to others for different situations. I take Iser to mean that literary works are similar to other social situations in that they also elicit alternate versions of ourselves, but with a difference.

The implied reader, the role I play or the self I become when reading, is created mainly by my interaction with the text. Normally while reading I would not consciously choose to emphasize one aspect or another of my identity, as I would upon walking into a faculty meeting or a classroom. Rather, I surrender the power of creation to the text, saying in effect, "Make of me what you will!" This is an act of great trust, but then, we trust novels—which may explain why we feel so betrayed by truly bad ones. We trust novels because they are play, much as we trust ourselves to the rules of *Monopoly*, believing that the self we become playing the game is not the self we must continue to be when the game is complete. Furthermore, our experience of novels is that the selves we become while reading are usually more interesting and often better than the selves we are usually allowed to be.

Though I do not use the term *implied reader* often until near the end of this study, I want to digress briefly to emphasize the importance of the concept in two ways. First, the rereading in the following chapters is largely an attempt to articulate the implied reader of *The Turn of the Screw,* to make clear that reader's major features as they seem to emerge from the text. Second, the implied reader concept is crucial to explaining how it is possible to read a truly ambiguous text. This text is truly ambiguous in that it seems to contain two mutually exclusive readings. If this description is accurate, then the implied reader of this story is likely to be absolutely ambivalent, unable to affirm one reading and exclude the other. Such a reader would be trapped, for unless one reading can be found, the reader must perpetually vibrate between the two. Imagine this analogy. You begin a *Monopoly* game and adopt the persona (implied reader) of a ruthless capitalist, ruining and humiliating your friends. Then, by some magic, you are condemned to play this game in this way continuously forever. The game would have captured and transformed your identity, depriving you of freedom and threatening you with madness. If the absolute ambiguity of *The Turn of the Screw* prevents us from concluding the process of reading, then this book's magic may entrap us readers in a disturbing role. The implied reader concept suggests how this trap may work. We will eventually discuss how the same concept may suggest ways of escaping the trap.

Reading, then, is the interaction of the reader and the text during which the reader responds to structures built into the text to create provisional wholes and move toward seeing the work as a whole. By participating in this interaction, the reader constructs as well an implied reader, a version of the self who is the appropriate reader of this work. This process takes place at two moments. The first is the first reading, when the reader moves through the text for the first time without any certain foreknowledge of what follows. In this reading we attempt to remember all that has passed, not only on the page, but in our constructions based on the language. We also project forward in the text, speculating on future parts and wholes. The second moment is all subsequent readings. All readings after the first are alike in that they attempt to bring to bear upon the reading experience the maximum that can be remembered from previous readings about what else is in the text.

Though in the following chapters I sometimes attempt to reconstruct the perspective of a first reading, I concentrate upon rereading, the kind of reading that takes place when we return from the death of Miles to the beginning of the text in the hope of resolving the ambiguity of the meaning of his death and the larger ambiguity that arises from it, the problem of the governess's character. I assume that upon this reading, the entire text and all reasoning about it can be brought to bear on interpreting any part of it.

This method of rereading is not an unusual approach. I emphasize it here only because I intend to do it in a self-conscious and systematic way, distinguishing with some care on occasion between first reading and rereading. To complete the introduction and to begin to illustrate the importance of this distinction, I turn now to some of the major features that seem to become important as we reread *The Turn of the Screw*.

The first reading of *The Turn of the Screw* is likely, but not certain, to be as a thriller. The prologue leads us to expect a ghost story that will "one up" the story of Griffin's ghost. The first reading will most likely produce an effect, like that described in the first phase of criticism of the tale, in which the ghosts are real and the governess good. In this reading the governess's reliability is assumed, and our attention is focused on what she reports. But, when we begin to wonder how the governess knows Miles is saved, and we reread with that question in mind, we become much more interested in the governess's character and her manner of telling. We need to assess her as a perceiver, a reporter, and a moral consciousness. To learn whether the governess is correct in her assertion that Miles gains his soul while losing his life, we must evaluate her ability to make such a judgment.

Upon rereading, certain features of the narration that were

probably in the background of the reader's attention upon first reading move into the foreground. Most of these are discussed in detail in subsequent chapters, but here I want to call attention to two features that govern the rereading: the governess's temporal perspective on her tale and the history of the development of her document.

The governess tells her tale from a perspective distant in time from the events themselves, in fact, more than ten years distant. Furthermore, this is her second telling, for first she told it aloud to Douglas, then wrote it out for him. This fact has a number of important implications. One of the most important has to do with the governess's lies.

A number of the psychoanalytic readings of the tale depend upon assertions that the governess tells lies. Some readers even try to see her as like the narrator of *The Aspern Papers,* who frankly reports himself as lying. For example, she is said to lie when she asserts that she conversed with the apparition of Miss Jessel in the schoolroom on the Sunday Miles requested that he be given more freedom (60). The governess's perspective of more than ten years and her second telling in the writing make such assertions extremely problematic. If she tells such obvious lies unconsciously at the time of the events, how do we account for her not catching herself in those lies during at least one of her tellings? If she tells them consciously, how can she report them to Douglas, orally or in writing, without judging them as she judges the morality of a number of her acts? And if they are obviously lies, why does Douglas never catch her up on them? Though these questions may be answered in ways that allow one to continue asserting that she reports herself as lying, it becomes much more difficult than some have thought to assert she lies when, upon rereading, we attend to the chronological perspective of her telling. It is immensely complicated to tell lies deliberately and then report them later as if they were unconscious. And, for the governess it is just as complicated to tell unconscious lies and report them twice more than ten years later to a discriminating listener without someone calling attention to them.

Attending to the circumstances of the governess's narration, while it does not reduce the possibility that she makes mistakes, virtually eliminates the possibility that she lies—unless her entire narration is a fabrication, as Edna Kenton argues. In this latter case, we would have quite a different book from what most readers have taken it to be, though many of the problems of interpreting it would remain the same. Realizing the governess's narrative position leads to one other implication I want to emphasize.

Because years have passed between the events and their telling, the governess has had much time to think about them, to consider their meaning. We can see in her first sentence that she has considered carefully not only the events themselves, but also the problem of how to recount them to someone else. This means that the governess has had time for, and shows actual evidence of, developing a comparatively objective perspective upon her adventures. Indeed, there is evidence that she has moved from a less organized outpouring of her story in the oral presentation to Douglas to a more careful, written presentation. For example, she repeatedly refers to her desire to be clear in her writing, and she often addresses Douglas directly, sometimes apparently in response to questions she remembers him asking in their exchanges. Her story has been thought over for years, then talked over, then thought over again before and during her writing.

Upon rereading we see clearly the governess's temporal distance from the events she narrates. Another important feature is the history of the development of her narrative—the ten-year delay, the oral telling, and the writing addressed to Douglas. These circumstances lead us to expect that she will show some mature and objective judgment of her perceptions, interpretations, and actions. As a result, we notice the judgments she made at the time of the events and the evaluations she makes of those judgments when she tells her story.

That the governess's narration is a carefully considered retelling becomes quite important when we reread. We notice this feature at the outset of the second reading, for most of the information that reveals it is in the prologue. Knowing that she has been over her interpretation several times is a kind of promise that we will find evidence of her worrying the story. Even though the promise of more information draws us into rereading in the hope of discovering the truth about

Miles's fate, this promise also raises new questions. I will mention only one here: why is the governess so worried about her story?

Upon first reading we probably think little about her motives for telling her story. She seems to be merely a stage prop used by James as a part of the machinery for telling a thrilling tale of terror. But, when we come to end of the tale, we realize that we were not reading merely a thrilling tale. A child has been killed, one presented as charming, talented, and lovable. A governess who professes deep love for that child was the only human agent present when he died. She has been presented as sensitive, intelligent, loyal, desperate, and troubled. We have come to care deeply about these characters, not merely as devices to bring horrors before us, but as fully realized characters whose fates seem important. At this point in the story, it is not enough to have had thrills and to have seen horrors. We want to comprehend the fates of these characters, to understand truly what has happened to them.

Because we care about the governess, we want to understand her. Central to the problem of understanding her is discovering her attitude toward her own story. Why does she delay telling it? Why does she choose Douglas as her listener and reader? Why does she tell her tale at all? In short, what does she want?

"The next night, by the corner of the hearth, in the best chair, he opened the faded red cover of a thin old-fashioned gilt-edged album. . . . But Douglas, without heeding me, had begun to read with a fine clearness that was like a rendering to the ear of the beauty of his author's hand" (6).

Illustration by Eric Pape, from *Collier's Weekly* 20, no. 17 (27 January 1898):21. Courtesy of the New York State Historical Association Library.

5

Perspectives in the Prologue

Repetitions: The Chasm of Death and the Master Reader

The prologue begins at the end of a provocative, strange story, told in front of a fire in an old English country house in the Christmas season. The narrator sketches briefly the tale of Griffin's ghost: "The case, I may mention, was that of an apparition in just such an old house as had gathered us for the occasion—an appearance, of a dreadful kind, to a little boy sleeping in the room with his mother and waking her up in the terror of it; waking her not to dissipate his dread and soothe him to sleep again, but to encounter also herself, before she had succeeded in doing so, the same sight that had shocked him" (1). This seemingly trivial story actually reverberates through the prologue and the whole tale, but first it provokes Douglas to reveal his long-kept secret.

Let us notice some of the elements of this ghost story. The listeners agree that it is especially gruesome because the ghost appears first to a little boy "at so tender an age." Were the ghost merely a nightmare, the event would not even be unusual. The way the listeners approach the story and the way it is told suggest that these people expect horrors to be imaginary, for children to experience them as dreams, and for adults to dissipate them, assuring children of their true safety from the supernatural. The gruesomeness of the tale results from its reversal of these expectations. The ghost awakens the child and the child awakens the mother to the ghost. By means of the child, the mother encounters terror to which she and her culture deny reality.

This story, which is about a repetition, begins to repeat itself when Douglas finally responds to it. As the narrator notes, Douglas takes some time to "awaken." She sees he has been stirred by Griffin's tale and that some response is imminent. Later in the evening, he announces that he has a story to tell that is in itself a more intense repetition of Griffin's story, a tale in which ghosts appear to two children. Beneath this most obvious repetition is another less obvious one. Douglas claims he is the only person to have heard the tale before, and he proposes to pass it on to his listeners. They simply anticipate entertainment. Douglas is like the child who claims to have seen a horror, and his announcement of the tale suggests that like the child, he looks for comfort. His audience is like the mother, not believing there will be anything substantial to encounter, just another fiction in the vein of Ann Radcliffe.

Upon rereading, the prologue calls attention to multiple repetitions that may not have seemed so important upon first reading. They point to James's manipulation of perspective in the prologue and raise questions about the functions of the perspectives James creates. A perspective here means no more than a point of view. For example, in the first few pages of the prologue we see several perspectives on Griffin's ghost story. Most of those present see it as mere entertainment. For Douglas it is an awakening spark.

We see upon rereading how the governess's narrative repeats the story of Griffin's ghost in several ways. In her narrative children open her eyes to ghostly apparitions. At least the children seem to be the reason for the appearances. She has told this story to Douglas, and the effect upon him has been shocking. He has remained silent about it for forty years. Now, under the provocation of Griffin's story and probably the presence of the narrator, Douglas has decided to retell the story. Insofar as we can determine, the effect of Douglas's telling upon the narrator is also shocking. She gives us this prologue, which contains a kind of implicit epilogue, but there is no formal epilogue, no indication of how she responds to Douglas's tale except the bare acts of introducing and presenting it to us. In a sense she too is frozen into a silence out of which emerges her repetition of the tale.

Upon rereading we encounter the significant pattern of the repeated message. As Shoshana Felman has suggested, this pattern pervades *The Turn of the Screw*.[7] For the governess, the story—that is, the conflict—originates in a letter addressed to the uncle but read by her, which announces Miles's expulsion from school. This letter reveals the possibility of a secret at Bly. Similarly, the narrative originates for us readers as a manuscript, a sort of letter addressed to Douglas, which upon first reading has suggested the possibility of a secret about the governess. Felman traces this repetition to other letters written during the governess's stay. The pattern leads in other directions as well, producing a chain of similar communications, beginning with the ghosts who supposedly communicated with Miles. Miles said "things" to the school fellows he liked. They repeated these to the masters who repeated them to the headmaster. The headmaster read in these "things" a secret that was serious enough to cause him to expel Miles and to remain silent about what he read. He wrote to the uncle, who refused to read this missive and sent it to the governess. She tried to read it "into" events at Bly, either by discovering or creating the ghosts. Then she told her story and wrote her "letter" to Douglas, who first read it to the prologue narrator, then gave it to her. The prologue narrator finally presents it to us. This chain of communication, by pointing at but not revealing a silent secret, suggests what other aspects of the prologue and the tale as a whole will confirm: there is an invisible impulse that keeps this communication moving, an impulse that seems to originate with the dead and that, as Felman argues, seeks a nonexistent master reader.

As rereaders, we remember the governess describing that equivocal last event—Miles dead and dispossessed in her arms—and we return to the prologue looking for the secret truth about this event. The prologue, by pointing to the repeated but silent message, confirms that there is something to be discovered. Someone knows the truth, but who? A glance at the chain of messages makes quite clear who knows the truth—the dead. Miles knows whether or not his heart is dispossessed, if the dead can know anything. Just as the chain of communication seems to begin with the dead talking to Miles, so the information that we—and perhaps others—want is possessed by the dead. To elaborate this idea more carefully, let us return to the pattern of repeated tellings of the governess's narrative, this time in the context of a chronology.

Chronology of Tellings of the Governess's Narrative

Year 1
Events at Bly take place.

Year 10
The governess tells her story to Douglas.

Year 30 (almost)
The governess sends Douglas her written narrative.

Year 30
The governess dies.

Year 50: Christmas Tuesday
Douglas announces the manuscript's existence.

Year 50: Christmas Thursday
Douglas begins to read the narrative.

Some time later
Douglas gives the manuscript to the narrator.

Soon afterward
Douglas dies.

Some time later
The narrator publishes the manuscript.

One obvious characteristic of this chronology is the delay between the various hearings and tellings. Delay indicates that this story is not mere entertainment, like that of Griffin's ghost. These people have been moved by it, confirming that it contains some powerful secret. Delay also indicates mystery. Why do the various narrators wait so long to retell the story? And if they are so reluctant, why do they tell it at all, and why does one telling seem, always after a delay, to beget another? These questions are answerable, but for the moment, let us consider what the dead may know.

A death precedes each telling: Miles's, the governess's, and Douglas's. These deaths suggest, among other ideas, a parallel between the message and the children. Just as a narrative in letter form is passed from reader to reader, the children are passed from parents to parents. When their natural parents die, apparently in India, the children go to their grandparents, who also die in India two years later. Then the children come to England where they are put under the care of Quint and Jessel, who soon die. The narrator notices this pattern as Douglas has and wonders whether caring for these children might have been life threatening (5). That the children, when they appear, prove silent on the subjects of death and the dead and especially the return of the dead, suggests that this parallel is significant.

The children are noticeably silent on a subject of some importance to them, for they have lost three sets of parents in a short time. Like the "things" and the manuscript, they have been passed, with their increasingly portentous silence, from one set of caretakers to another. If the dead know the secret and have communed with the children, then perhaps the children know.

The story of Griffin's ghost becomes a paradigm for the whole novella. The child awakens the parent to a vision of the dead returned, and the vision proves persistent, thus "awakening" the parent as well. The something that keeps this story moving from one teller to another is the very fact that it carries with it a silent secret. If once that secret were spoken, perhaps the chain of retellings would end. If once we knew the truth about Miles and the governess, we could complete our rereading.

For the reader the children become, as they were for the governess, a source of knowledge. We readers discover ourselves in the position of wishing to repeat what the governess has done. She has discovered that the children know a secret, that they have communed with the dead, and she has decided for complicated reasons to read that secret and to act upon what she reads. Likewise, we have discovered that the governess has a secret. Returning to the prologue, we see more clearly the apparent movement of that secret from the dead speaking to Miles through a chain of communications, and finally into the manuscript we are about to reread. As the governess found it necessary to read the children in order to understand how she should act toward them, so we find it necessary to read them and her to learn how to judge her and, thus, the truth about their fate. The governess, standing between the reader and the children, remains the reader's sole source of knowledge about the children.

Within the prologue, then, the supposed knowledge of the children becomes a means of discovering what lurks behind the delays and the repetitions of the governess's narrative. Douglas's silence and his eventual outbreak focus the reader on mystery, to which the children and, therefore, the governess may possess clues. The reader's problem is defined as reading the governess's reading of the children. The problem of reading people is central to the entire tale.

This problem is accentuated by death. We have only texts to deal with. Their authors are all dead: Miles, the governess, Douglas, and, since 1916, James and his narrator. James left some commentary, which has proven equivocal when critics have tried to find authority in it. James knew well the maddening absoluteness of the abyss of death. According to Leon Edel, James experienced this barrier deeply upon the death of his friend, Constance Fenimore Woolson.

Woolson died in Venice on 24 January 1894. She and James had been intimate, perhaps even living together briefly. Edel believes she expected James to marry her after the death of his sister, Alice, in 1892, but instead James distanced himself. Alone, depressed, and perhaps delirious with influenza, Woolson threw herself from an upper-story window. Naturally, this death left troubling questions in James's mind. Did she commit suicide? Was he at all responsible? He said in a letter, "There is much that is tragically obscure in that horror of last week—and I feel as if I were living in the shadow of it."[8] Edel points out that in 1895 James wrote two stories in which people carry greatly desired knowledge into death with them: "The Figure in the Carpet" and "The Friends of the Friends."[9] To his list we might add at least two other stories with a strongly realized similar theme: "The Altar of the Dead" (1895) and "The Beast in the Jungle" (1903).

This theme seems central as well to *The Turn of the Screw*. Only Miles certainly knows what we want to know. But the dead remain silent, leaving us to speak for them as we may. Hence the search for a master reader, for someone living who can speak authoritatively for this silence.

The problem presented pointedly in the prologue upon rereading, then, is to find a perspective from which the silent and invisible will become articulate and visible. Between us readers and the information we desire is the chasm of death. We have before us written testimony. Can we find within this testimony an authoritative perspective that will allow us to assert with some degree of certainty that we have spoken for silence, envisioned the invisible?

The prologue provides illustrations of this problem and a number of perspectives that we may examine.

MIRRORS

The problem of reading to discover the silent and invisible leads us to another important pattern in the prologue and the tale as a whole, the mirror pattern. Christine Brooke-Rose describes a mirror structure that pervades the governess's narration.[10] She argues that the governess arrives at Bly with an incomplete, fragmented self. Seeing her body whole for the first time in the full-length mirrors at Bly, the governess comes to desire psychic wholeness. This desire cannot be realized until she is able to recognize and accept her unconscious desires for power and sexual gratification. In her actions at Bly the governess fails to put herself together. Instead, she projects herself onto most of the other characters: the morally innocent self onto the children; the repressed, guilty self onto the ghosts; and the rational, skeptical self onto Mrs. Grose. By implication the governess fails to understand what she does, whether or not there are real ghosts present. Another implication of Brooke-Rose's analysis is that in turning to Douglas the governess continues to look for a mirror, a person who will see her whole and love her.

I am talking about mirrors of a psychological kind. Part of becoming a free and powerful adult is self-mastery. We try to achieve a state of consciousness in which our actions are chosen by us rather than for us. By choosing our actions freely, we hope to gain control over our destinies and to give a shape to our lives that will eventuate in fulfillment and satisfaction. One of the ironies of the human condition is that any individual knows himself or herself only from within. I can know myself from the outside only by examining the opinions of others who know me. Looking into a mirror, I can glimpse a view of my person unavailable from within. By sharing another person's perspective, I can gain a view of my identity not possible from inside. A further irony of human nature is that even when I look into a mirror or share another's perception, I am still looking from inside myself. From that position I cannot easily determine whether the other's view is accurate or even whether I have correctly interpreted the other's view.

Brooke-Rose has suggested that the governess comes to desire self-mastery and that in her first attempts to find herself at Bly, she falls into projection. Projection in this case is a two-sided form of identification. On the one hand, she consciously identifies with the children and willingly enters into the absolute goodness and innocence she sees in them. On the other hand, she unconsciously denies aspects of herself she cannot easily accommodate, projecting her unacceptable and impossible sexual desires upon the ghosts. She makes ghosts and children into mirrors, but these mirrors do not reflect her whole self back to her, because she is unaware of what she is doing. She sees two sets of unrelated images, while we see reflections of her psychological state. Her perception that the ghosts want to get at the children provides us with a further link between the opposing reflections, and we infer her unconscious fear that the repressed self will overcome her conscious self.

Perspectives in the Prologue

Using others as mirrors is one way of discovering the silent and invisible in oneself. In *The Turn of the Screw* we readers depend upon the governess's attempt to know herself. Like her text, the governess desires a master reader or a master mirror. We can easily see why this is true. If she is sensitive at all, then she must also arrive at the doubts we discover at the end of her narrative. She must also wonder whether she really saved Miles. Since only Miles knows the answer and he has crossed the silent chasm of death, the governess can only look into herself for an answer. But she cannot see her whole self. This may be the position from which she turns to Douglas with her story. She gives him all the relevant facts at her disposal and by implication asks his opinion. She asks Douglas to be her mirror. In this choice she is like any person who wonders how to evaluate her actions and turns to a trusted friend for advice.

In the prologue James illustrates the powers and limitations of using others as mirrors of oneself. In the interchanges between Douglas and the prologue narrator, we see repeated attempts at mirroring. Whenever one character fills in the blank of an incomplete idea or answers the question of another, mirroring may take place. One character arrives at something he cannot yet say, and the other tries to say it. When the exchange is successful, the two are temporarily of one mind; love and intimacy are sustained. But when they fail, they emphasize and must face their inevitable separation. The progress of attempts at mirroring in the prologue shows that while mirroring is often successful and does sustain intimacy, ultimately it must fail. No person can fully and consistently mirror another. This realization bodes ill for our wish to become master readers.

In the first paragraph of the prologue, the narrator reports that on the evening she learned of Douglas's story, she watched him with care. Her first inferences prove correct, that Douglas was struck by the Griffin story and that this would lead to his telling a story. Her next inference, however, seems to lead to an error. She says, "our friend, with quiet art, prepared his triumph by turning his eyes over the rest of us and going on" (1). She implies that she saw him then as intending to entertain them with this tale. She defines this entertainment as

45

"sheer terror," but he then seems to respond artlessly, from the heart:

> He seemed to say it was n't so simple as that; to be really at a loss how to qualify it. He passed his hand over his eyes, made a little wincing grimace. "For dreadful—dreadfulness!"
> "Oh how delicious!" cried one of the women.
> He took no notice of her; he looked at me, but as if, instead of me, he saw what he spoke of. "For general uncanny ugliness and horror and pain." (1–2)

It is possible that Douglas is highly artful, but the narrator at least momentarily doubts that his performance is the product of art, for he seems really moved. He pointedly rejects the interpretation of "one of the women," which is also the interpretation of the narrator. Upon her first error of reading, the narrator sees herself mirrored in Douglas's eye, as if she were "what he spoke of": ugliness and horror and pain. To misread and fail as a mirror is to become the horror Douglas associates with the governess's story.

At this point in the prologue Douglas seems to be seeing the narrator in the same way he has probably been seeing the governess since hearing her tale, as someone for whom he cares, but who also has an invisible, terrifying side that repeatedly manifests itself in various ways, one of which is a failure to mirror him as he has expected.

Another irony of mirroring appears in this failure. While it seems that the narrator has failed to mirror Douglas, she may actually have succeeded, though neither she nor Douglas could know this. It is possible that Douglas consciously takes his story very seriously while unconsciously harboring desires to entertain and to enjoy the center of attention. This possibility offers one way of explaining why the narrator seems to become horrifying to him when she apparently fails to mirror him. She may, in fact, show him a side of himself he has repressed. His horror may arise from having to face the truth that he and the narrator cannot be forever of one mind or from the glimpse she gives of his unacknowledged wishes. Either possibility could remind him of his reactions to the governess's narrative, for it may have had the effects of making the governess seem alien to him or of confronting him with his own conscious/unconscious split.

Failures at mirroring, then, can be unnerving on at least two levels, perhaps even simultaneously. They can reveal the limits of loving and also the reality and presence of the silent and invisible, unconscious self.

Despite the early failure of the narrator to take Douglas as seriously as he intends to be taken, he depends upon her as a mirror. He seems to appeal to the narrator for aid in breaking the ice of his forty-year silence. He assures her that she will easily judge why the governess told no one the story before telling him, and he praises her acuteness in perceiving that the governess was in love. In so depending upon the narrator, he assumes a closeness to her that reflects his relationship with the governess, in which much is communicated without being spoken. That relationship was characterized by reading and reflecting each other: "She had never told any one. It wasn't simply that she said so, but that I knew she had n't. I was sure; I could see. You'll easily judge why when you hear" (2). Here Douglas pointedly emphasizes the similarity of the two relationships.

Unspoken secrets also repeatedly intrude into communications between the narrator and Douglas, because she is inevitably an imperfect mirror and because Douglas cannot ultimately be read. Douglas and the narrator seem to read and reflect each other perfectly when Douglas correctly completes her thought about the "necessary danger to life" of the position at Bly, and when they agree on the beauty of the governess's passion. Still, their relationship is last seen equivocally. The narrator asserts that she has a title for his narrative. By implication, this is *The Turn of the Screw,* but we never actually learn what her title is. Douglas ignores this suggestion and begins to mirror in his voice the governess's handwriting. The narrator's assertion of a title for a narrative she has not yet heard and for which Douglas has no title underlines at the end of the prologue the persisting division between them over whether Douglas's preparation for the narrative is artful or heartfelt. On the first evening, even after she has been made to doubt that he is merely artful and after she has decided that he really has overcome "his reasons for a long silence," she joins with the other listeners, in Douglas's absence, in expecting a "tremendous occasion" when the story is told (3). Together with her assertion of a title, this remark suggests that, at least until she actually heard the tale, she continued to think of it as an entertaining fiction rather than a confession that could adequately account for Douglas's real pain as well as for his desire to unburden himself after forty years. Written after Douglas's death, the narrator's prologue cannot resolve this question. Ultimately, death shatters even the best mirror.

Mirroring between persons is one path to self-knowledge, and we must depend upon the governess's self-discovery in her narrative. If we find little evidence of deep self-awareness, then we may conclude that she is most likely mistaken in her hope that she saved Miles. But if we see that she is seeking self-awareness in the mirrors of others, then we must try to determine whether she has discovered the truth. That each hearer of her tale lapses into silence from which emerges not an explanation, but a repetition of the story indicates that no one has yet achieved the role of master reader.

Barriers and Perspectives

In a room, inside a box, is an object. We are forbidden entrance into the room, but we desire to observe the object. The room has a number of doors and windows through which we may look. Perhaps through one of these openings we will be able to see a chink in the box, so we try each one, hoping for a glimpse of that object. This is a picture of our problem in rereading *The Turn of the Screw,* as I have described it so far. The box is death and has no chinks, unless the dead really do return and speak to us. The room is the past to which we cannot return. The windows and doors are provided by the text, which we have come to look at, upon rereading, as a record of people observing and interpreting. These observers and interpreters are our windows and doors. To see the object in the box, we must cross at least three levels of barriers: the observers, the past, and death.

Perspectives in the Prologue

These barriers should lead rational minds to despair. Fortunately for the future of *The Turn of the Screw*, we are not rational when we read this book. The first reading was probably undertaken in the spirit of risky play; the second is driven by the passion to know all. Therefore, we care not that the wall of death is impenetrable, that the past is inaccessible, and that, therefore, we are thrown upon the tenuous authority of our observers. Indeed, we cling to our observers, for they are our only means of meeting the challenge of interpretation presented by this tale. They are our hope, and because they are several, they are a kind of promise. If there are many perspectives, then perhaps one or some combination will achieve authority, revealing a chink in the box.

The prologue, upon rereading, offers at least eight perspectives on the events.

The Eight Main Perspectives in the Prologue

The governess	• The events at Bly
	• Writing her account
Douglas	• Hearing the governess's story at his home
	• Reading it during the Christmas gathering
The narrator	• Hearing Douglas's reading
	• Publishing the manuscript (silent reaction)
The reader	• The first reading
	• Subsequent readings

The governess presents two main perspectives: how events appeared at the time they occurred and her position at the time she writes her narrative. Intervening between them is the perspective of her first telling Douglas. He fills in this point of view in the prologue; hints of that occasion appear in the governess's narrative. Douglas's second perspective is when he presents the narrative to his friends. This is the occasion of the prologue narrator's first point of view, her initial reaction to Douglas's presentation. She creates a second, but silent perspective by publishing the manuscript. Not revealing in words how she responded to the presentation, she simply acts, producing a prologue and reproducing the text. These perspectives invite the reader to see the tale from six points of view and to imaginatively occupy five different times: the events themselves, the governess's telling, her writing, Douglas's repetition, and the narrator's repetition. Out of these perspectives we construct our first reading and the rereadings.

By rereading, the reader enters into the pattern of repetition. At this moment, as you read these words, you occupy the implicit perspective toward which the prologue invites you. By coming this far, you have entered into the pattern of the repeated message as you repeat it to yourself, trying to turn it over and read its underside.

These eight perspectives do not exhaust those suggested by the text. We have not mentioned the author's perspective. As many readers have noted, James's absence from the text as an "objective" narrative voice is a key cause of the tale's ambiguity. James is present as implied author at those parts of the prologue in which the reader questions the narrator's judgments. He is silently present in the governess's narrative when her language reveals elements of which she is unconscious, for example, perhaps, in some of the more sophisticated wordplay. He is also available extratextually as a commentator on the tale in his prefaces and other writings. Though any of these perspectives may be brought to bear in our rereading, the eight in the table seem the main ones offered by the text.

The barriers of death, time, and filtering minds between the "events" and the reader's encounter with the text may be seen as challenges to be overcome and, therefore, as appropriate to the sort of tale Mrs. Griffin expects. But, these five temporal locations and the perspectives they generate work differently. They are not present to the reader in the same way the barriers are. The invitations to adopt perspectives and to occupy imaginative positions are not obstacles at all, but offers of help. The invitations are subtle; the reader's response is likely to be simply to accept rather than to notice and question as we do when we step back from the reading or rereading process in criticism. And it is surprising and shocking to discover that by accepting these invitations, the reader implicitly, even before reconsidering the narrative, accepts the impossibilities of reading the unreadable and of making silence speak.

The prologue leads the reader into adopting a plural perspective on the governess's experience. Furthermore, it sets up a situation in which it becomes impossible to reject any of the perspectives, even Mrs. Griffin's. There is no perspective from which to rule out categorically the possibility that Douglas or the narrator created the whole story, that one of them is, in effect, James. The history of the criticism of this text indicates that there is no master perspective from which any other in the text can be absolutely affirmed or rejected. Even James's extratextual commentary has proven less than authoritative.

The prologue reveals relationships among the various perspectives that increase the difficulty of according superior authority to any one of them. We have seen at several points in the chain of communications that affection is offered as the motive for passing the message. If telling the story is an act of love, then the reader may be assumed to be the recipient of affection. The request to participate in these perspectives would then be an invitation to engage in an act of love. A lover cannot reject part of the beloved without rejecting the whole person: to love is to accept the whole perspective of the other, whether or not one shares it. Readers may not consciously experience themselves as loved by the characters who provide these perspectives, but nevertheless they are in the position of loved ones, for the characters are the sole sources of the readers' viewpoints. To reject a perspective is not, then, simply a matter of deciding who is right and who is wrong, but becomes a matter of rejecting or accepting differing perspectives linked by love. Not only are none of the perspectives authoritative, but also all of them belong to lovers and beloveds.

The eight main perspectives belong to four people: the governess, Douglas, the narrator, and the reader. There are eight because each person is split between two moments, the moment of experience and the moment of reflection or telling. Between each of these pairs of moments is a period of silence, of aloneness with oneself, out of which emerges the second moment, which, with the possible exception of the rereading, involves giving the moment of experience to another. The act of giving emphasizes the importance of the period of silence and indicates a deeper split in the giver, for that pause of silence gives rise to doubt, and doubt impels the repetition of the story. We readers want most to know what transpires in that silence.

The governess's narrative may be seen as a reflection on the self she was at Bly, in which case she may be concerned with whether that self deserves love. If she saved Miles, she deserves to be loved. If she killed him, perhaps she does not. Her dilemma is that she can never know what she did. If she tells Douglas in order to solve her dilemma, she fails, for he is silenced. Nevertheless, he continues to love her. Douglas, too, is split into the self who heard her story and the self who finally retells it forty years later. The narrator is split in time in the same way, though we know less about what differences there may be between the two versions of her self. Finally, the reader is split at the end of the tale between the two possible stories in the governess's narrative.

If each of the persons has two perspectives, to choose one is to reject the other, for this temporal split is the result of a more fundamental split between the conscious and the unconscious, the articulate and the silent.

Each person sees a reflection of the self in the other, and in at least three cases, the other is a lover or beloved. To see a split there is to remember a split in the perceiving self, as we observed when Douglas saw the narrator as "the horror." When another seems to fail to mirror oneself, one may suspect that an invisible side of oneself is appearing. Although being caught in ambiguity is painful, it is something like madness to finalize the split by casting away half of it. How does one reject one's unconscious with any finality? How does one erase one's past thoughts and actions from the book of the soul? While the four characters are bound by love, the split perspectives within them are bound by the human desire for psychic wholeness, the same desire that makes the split a source of anxiety. The only alternative remaining is to do what the three tellers and we rereaders find ourselves doing. We repeat the tale with its silence intact. We cannot grant final authority to any perspective.

Each teller repeats the tale in his or her fashion, revealing the public self and its shadow of silence, but never successfully speaking for that silence. To love oneself or another is to preserve the silence. The governess's tragic situation is highlighted when we realize this, for love seems to demand that she violate the silence of her little charges because their lives and souls are in danger. She can never know whether her speaking for silence saved Miles or killed him, for his reflective surface has vanished.

The reader naturally and unconsciously accepts the invitation to adopt the viewpoints offered in the prologue and, so, becomes enmeshed in the links of love and identity between those perspectives. These links bind the perspectives together without eliminating their separateness. The implied reader of *The Turn of the Screw* occupies a plurality of times and places and a multiplicity of perspectives as he or she returns to the governess's narrative. This reader reads with many eyes and imagines with many minds, and so never escapes the labyrinth of mystery. James seems to have wanted a rereader who could not easily impose an interpretation on the tale and who, therefore, could not easily violate any of its narrators.

Our next major concern must be the authority of the governess. I approach the problem of her authority from three main directions: her own perspectives, her interactions with the ghosts, and her treatment of the children.

6

A Novice Authority:
The Governess Reads Herself

The Whole Beginning

From the beginning the governess is concerned with wholes and patterns. She has seen her experiences at Bly whole and has found a pattern in the beginning, "a little see-saw of the right throbs and the wrong" (6). She is referring to her self-confidence, to what lifts it and what drops it. Douglas has said that the uncle's charm moved her to accept her first position, despite the location in an isolated country house and the unusual condition that she not bother the master. She says that the charm of the uncle's appearance caused her confidence to rise in town, but then her doubts "bristled again." In this state of doubt, she rode a bumping coach to a stopping place. Then her "fortitude revived" under the influence of better transportation, beautiful weather and scenery, and the welcome she received at Bly. Her belief that she could handle this job was sustained until the next day, when her doubts were renewed by a fuller appreciation of her responsibility. Her new circumstances prove to have "an extent and mass for which I had not been prepared" (9).

At the end of her second day at Bly, her feelings continue to hover between self-confidence and doubt, as can be seen in her three visions of the house. The girl Flora, she says, tends to lift her confidence, making the house seem "a castle of romance inhabited by a rosy sprite" (10). But she is well aware that it is really an ordinary, though large and reasonably comfortable old house. This world is real, and she is fully responsible. Her third vision captures her ambivalence: "I had the fancy of our being almost as lost as a handful of passengers in a great drifting ship. Well, I was strangely at the helm!" (10).

The governess is worried about her responsibility from the beginning. At twenty she is barely adult herself. The youngest of several children of a poor country parson, she has never seen the kind of life over which she must now rule alone, has never had a large bed, an expansive view, perhaps not even a room of her own. She has never seen herself full length in a mirror before. She wonders whether she can rise to the responsibility of directing the care of two children in such an establishment.

The governess, then, is a novice authority. In her own family she has been near the bottom of the structure of authority. Now, in a matter of days she finds herself at the head of what for her is a grand house. No wonder that she is anxious, that she vacillates between attraction to the power and freedom this job promises and fear at the responsibility it places upon her. Suddenly she is captain of a great ship.

Another change has taken place during the short time since she went to London in answer to the uncle's advertisement. She has apparently experienced her first passion. Indeed, this emotion is her primary motive in the beginning, for she would surely have refused this position had she not been "carried away" in London.

We have at the outset, then, a young woman without experience in the exercise of authority, unsure of herself, awed by the responsibility she has accepted, attracted by the consideration that comes with authority, and supported by a passion that determines her to try this difficult task despite her fears. What do these factors reveal about the governess's fitness for her job? That she lacks experience as a governess and as head of a household is a problem. Not only is she liable to errors that would ordinarily be corrected by parents or other authorities, but she might fall victim to the seductions of absolute power.

That she worries about those weaknesses shows a fair degree of self-possession, but it is no perfect protection from error. That she is attracted by the life she envisions at Bly is a promise of growth and fulfillment of her character, but again, this growth is unregulated by external authority. Her sense of order and the good must come from within. That she is in love for the first time has given her the courage to take a job that she would have declined in cool reason. Courage is admirable, but at what point might it pass into foolhardiness?

THE GOVERNESS UNDER A SPELL

As the governess settles in we see the features of her character develop and change. She quickly comes to see Mrs. Grose as a coauthority. She discovers that by loving and forming the children she can both fulfill her own life and deserve the uncle's appreciation. The beauty of the children and the resulting ease of caring for them cast what she calls a spell on her; she seems for a time actually to live in the house of romance she first saw under Flora's influence, a place where courage is not really needed. On one occasion before ghosts appear, however, her courage is tested—when she learns that Miles has been expelled from school.

Mrs. Grose and the governess immediately discover common ground in their full appreciation of Flora's beauty. Soon their relationship becomes similar to that between the prologue narrator and Douglas, as they finish each other's thoughts, usually but not always accurately: "There were naturally things that in Flora's presence could pass between us only as prodigious and gratified looks, obscure and roundabout allusions . . . One would n't, it was already conveyed between us, too grossly flatter a child" (8). When the governess says she was carried away in London, Mrs. Grose correctly guesses the event took place in Harley Street, where the uncle, their master, lives. In the early chapters, this mirroring fails most noticeably when Mrs. Grose speaks in the past tense of a man who liked women young and pretty. She almost certainly is speaking of Quint, the master's deceased valet, but she conceals this from the governess (12). The governess is soon convinced that they will be at one on every question, and she reflects as she composes her narration that this indeed proved a correct conclusion. We will see more evidence that their relationship is not so perfectly harmonious as the statement implies.

As an older woman with experience in caring for the house and for the children, Mrs. Grose can be depended upon to keep the governess's feet on the ground. But there are limits to her dependability. She is a simple, uneducated person who knows her place in the authority structure of the household. There is the danger that she will be too easily led to believe the assertions of an educated gentlewoman placed over her. Their initial harmony might easily prove a trap for Mrs. Grose. Furthermore, Mrs. Grose's authority becomes an issue, for she is also the governess's sole source of information about the children's past. Though she is reluctant to say so, Mrs. Grose dislikes Quint and Jessel, the deceased former governess, just as she idolizes the children.

While she serves the governess as a partial substitute for a higher authority against which to check her interpretations, Mrs. Grose does not serve us readers so well. She is too limited both in ability and in power to give us assurance that the governess's interpretations are correct. Mrs. Grose's agreement with the governess cannot be enough.

As the governess comes to know Bly and the children, she sees more completely how this job can fulfill her: "To watch, teach, 'form' little Flora would too evidently be the making of a happy and useful life" (8). She finds Miles equally wonderful, and when she decides not to send him to another school, she also undertakes "forming" him. Their beauty and innocence seem Edenic to her, "as if I had been in charge of a pair of little grandees, of princes of the blood, for whom everything, to be right, would have to be fenced about and ordered and arranged, the only form that in my fancy the after-years could take for them was that of a romantic, a really royal extension of the garden and the park" (15).

Forming the children takes on for her the character of protecting them from the world, from growing up into what she characterizes as "the rough future." Insofar as she adopts such an intention in reality, she is mistaken, but she emphasizes in her narration the recognition that futures are difficult and that her fancy was induced in part by the charming spell of the children. This notion indicates another possible weakness in her reading, for it suggests a point at which she might read herself into the children. Her life at this time seemed to be the Eden she dreamed for them; to preserve that world, she would need to keep them unchanged. From this point it is an easy step for her to identify the children with her "innocent" conscious self, free of the unconscious desires that can awaken upon falling in love and achieving authority.

The governess sums up her accomplishments before Quint's first appearance in this way: "It was a pleasure at these moments to feel myself tranquil and justified; doubtless perhaps also to reflect that by my discretion, my quiet good sense and general high propriety, I was giving pleasure—if he ever thought of it!—to the person to whose pressure I had yielded. What I was doing was what he had earnestly hoped and directly asked of me, and that I *could,* after all, do it proved even a greater joy than I had expected" (15). Her life is justified, and she is content. She is showing the qualities she thinks correct in her position, discretion and propriety. She is doing a valuable work well and giving pleasure to the master and to herself. She implies clearly that at the time this was almost enough. Her love for the uncle is fulfilled in so serving him, but she does wish he could know how well she is doing. Her need for the power and freedom to pursue her own fulfillment is more than satisfied, issuing in unexpected joy. Her anxiety about whether she can do the job is allayed.

These accomplishments confirm the governess's original motive. She came out of love for the master, and love for him and also for the children continues to sustain her. But there is a major problem with her feelings in the days before Quint's appearances. There is an element of deception, of which the governess has since become aware: "Oh it was a trap—not designed but deep—to my imagination, to my delicacy, perhaps to my vanity; to whatever in me was most excitable. The best way to picture it all is to say that I was off my guard" (14).

A Novice Authority: The Governess Reads Herself

She says she was "under a charm." This charm was largely the result of the innocence and social grace of the children. She says they gave her lessons in how to be amused and in accepting consideration. This spell kept her from looking ahead, from fully realizing that their current state could not last. She deceives herself about the consequences of her decision to do nothing about Miles's expulsion from school.

At the time of her writing, she is fully aware of this error, and she attributes it possibly in part to conceit: "What I look back at with amazement is the situation I accepted. . . . I found it simple, in my ignorance, my confusion and perhaps my conceit, to assume that I could deal with a boy whose education for the world was all on the point of beginning" (14). Though she is unsure about confessing conceit, she repeats the idea at least twice as she considers her error: she says that "sweet consideration" was a trap "perhaps to my vanity," and she says, "I dare say I fancied myself in short a remarkable young woman and took comfort in the faith that this would more publicly appear" (15).

Under the spell of her comparative success, the governess overlooks for a time the consequences of the way she has dealt with her first crisis, the letter announcing Miles's expulsion. Brooke-Rose points out that an important feature of the tale is the violation of an injunction.[11] The uncle has imposed the condition that she take charge of Bly and not bother him. This is the original injunction. When the governess receives the headmaster's letter, it comes with a specific instance of this injunction: "Read him please; deal with him; but mind you don't report. Not a word" (10). This places the governess in a double bind. She must eventually bother the master, though she manages to delay this violation until forced to send Flora to town. Since there is no reason given for Miles's expulsion, she can only assume the implied reason is unspeakable, for any ordinary reason such as overcrowding would probably be specified. And she apparently cannot solicit more information. It is not her place to communicate with a headmaster, but the uncle's. She can neither learn more specifically why Miles was expelled—except from Miles himself—nor find a new school for him without going back through the master. She cannot deal with the headmaster as instructed without bothering the master as she is forbidden to do.

The governess decides to do nothing in response to the letter. With this decision Mrs. Grose agrees, promising to stand by her and to see it out. That Mrs. Grose accepts and applauds what the governess later sees and points out as an error helps to undercut Mrs. Grose as a reliable validator of the governess's authority.

Why does the governess make this choice? She says she was "lifted aloft on a great wave of infatuation and pity" (14). This seems to mean she was unwilling to expose Miles to the unpleasantness of an inquiry and thereby break the delicious spell under which they lived together. The effect of her choice, at least, was to preserve a status quo that she—and everyone else so far as she knew—found quite agreeable. What she did not allow to be fully present to her mind at the time of this decision was that it could only be a postponement. Eventually, she would have to communicate with the uncle, telling him what is in the letter he refused to read.

Clearly, a cooler head would have made sure Miles could go to school next term. Such a course would probably amount to sacrificing her and Miles's immediate interests in favor of Miles's ultimate welfare, forcing the uncle to undergo the unpleasantness that, after all, really is his responsibility. The governess is well aware of this when she composes her narrative; she confesses she was off her guard, caught up in the vanity of thinking she is doing a good job because everything goes along pleasantly and smoothly. That she was off her guard carries with it the suggestion that she might have been expected eventually to wake up and pay attention. This awakening is forestalled, however, by the "spring of the beast," the apparitions. Once she learns of the ghosts, the problem of communicating with the master seems to become much more complex.

Examining the governess's character as it appears in her actions before the ghosts appear both supports and undercuts the authority of her perceptions and interpretations. That Miles has been accused of causing injury to the other students at his school is probable, but her belief has no supporting authority. That she falls into the error of thinking she is doing a good job and deserves praise despite her failure to deal satisfactorily with Miles's school problem shows her quite capable of being deceived and of participating willingly in her own deception. That Mrs. Grose acquiesces in these errors reveals the absence of a reliable check on the governess. On the other hand, love remains at the center of her motives. Her love for Miles makes the implicit charge against him impossible to believe. Her love for the uncle inclines her toward not disturbing him if it can be managed. Her errors arise from her virtues as well as her weaknesses. Equivocation about her character remains possible even before she begins seeing "things."

THE ART I NOW NEED TO MAKE IT A LITTLE DISTINCT: THE GOVERNESS TALKS TO DOUGLAS

One other element in the governess's introduction of herself seems important to determining her authority as an interpreter. Though we are quite interested in how good an interpreter she was when the events took place, we are also concerned to understand how she interprets herself from her more mature perspective as she composes her narrative. One of the most important features of her opening chapters is the clear presence of her mature consciousness. We see her organizing and evaluating while consciously under the loving but questioning eye of Douglas.

We have already observed several instances of the governess's perspective at the time she composes her narration. In most of these we can also catch a personal, conversational tone that implies an awareness of Douglas, her reader. She is aware of herself as rereading Bly and in the process examining her perceptions and interpretations from a different and more mature point of view. She begins by saying she has an interpretation of these events to offer, that she has seen it whole and has found patterns of order. We have seen her make explicit judgments of deficiencies and errors that she sees from her new perspective: of her inexperience, her excitability, her vanity, her liability to deception, and her error in letting the ship drift under the charm of pleasure in the children's company. She points to her inexperience just before giving her first three views of the house: "I have not seen Bly since the day I left it, and I dare say to my present older and more informed eyes it would show a very reduced importance" (9). She is quite aware that her current interpretation differs from her initial interpretation, and she seems willing to point out these differences to Douglas.

Taking note of points at which she refers to her writing reveals several features of the governess's more mature point of view; one of the most important concerns the motive of her narrative. For example, she confesses her anxiety before arriving at Bly about getting along with Mrs. Grose, "a relation over which ... I fear I had rather brooded" (7). At this early point in the story, this is quite a minor comment, but it reveals a confessional tone. When she says "I fear," she is speaking of her feelings at the moment of writing, not of how she felt while traveling to Bly. When she says she fears that she brooded, she acknowledges that from her present point of view, she recognizes that Douglas would consider such brooding as perhaps childish and inappropriate. From this moment to the end of her narrative, she continues frankly to confess to faults and errors as she sees them. Some of these are quite serious, as we see in her self-deception over the problem of Miles's school.

One of her motives in retelling her story, then, is to tell the truth. That she is willing to confess her faults and errors shows that the truth is more important to her than simply looking good to Douglas. Another indication of her desire to get at the truth is her repeated concern with the difficulty of being clear. She finds it so hard to explain her earlier spellbound state that it reminds her "of all the art I now need to make it a little distinct" (14).

Furthermore, her repeating that she must strive to be clear and that this requires art should remind us that in writing her story, she is telling it a second time and that in reading it, Douglas is presumably going over it at least for the second time. By writing, she is reenacting those summer afternoons with Douglas when she first told him this story. She must at this point remember Douglas's first reactions and respond to them.

To illustrate the influence of this previous telling on the composition of the manuscript, let us note a remark she makes while describing Quint's first appearance: "The great question, or one of these, is afterwards, I know, with regard to certain matters, the question of how long they have lasted" (17). This is quite a surprising sentence where it appears. Upon first reading it almost makes no sense, for it is the first indication that Quint is not merely a strange man, but rather a ghostly apparition. During James's career spiritualism and various attempts at scientific research into "spirit phenomena" became increasingly popular. Such authorities as William James, Henry's older brother, and major public figures as Sir Arthur Conan Doyle were involved in psychical research. And, of course, the scientific approach to such phenomena led to the standard question "How long did it last?" Though the governess's experiences and her narration predate the establishment of formal scientific interest in the occult, *The Turn of the Screw* was published when the trend was in flood. Contemporary readers would have immediately recognized the significance of this sentence and would have understood that this strange man is the ghost the prologue prepared us to find.

That this sentence appears before the governess reveals her own discovery that the man is Quint, who is dead, implies fairly directly her previous telling. Of course, she knows that the stranger is Quint's ghost, but in putting this sentence here, she also acknowledges that Douglas shares this knowledge with her. Furthermore, she may imply that it was Douglas who asked how long it lasted. To even raise such a question in this particular context is to recognize a need that is not her own, for the duration of Quint's appearance is of little significance to its meaning. For this reason the question seems likely to have come from the only person ever to have heard her story before, a person who is not, however, present as she writes, Douglas.

On the other hand, the governess is not perfectly consistent in treating Douglas as if he has already heard her oral narrative. For example, in chapter 10 she directly addresses Douglas in ways that imply he does not know what will follow and that request his sympathy for her sufferings. She says that if she had then overcome her scruples and spoken with Flora about the apparitions she might have spared herself, "well, you'll see what" (43). She goes on to say that after she had found Flora awake at her window at midnight, "You may imagine the general complexion . . . of my nights" (43). This inconsistency may be explained in several ways, but the main point to notice is that the governess is at least sometimes aware of having more than once revised her interpretation.

When describing her first view of Quint, she says, "So I saw him as I see the letters I form on this page" (17). Having reread the prologue, we are quite sensitive to the other meaning of "letters." We remember the chain of unreadable communications originating with the dead. In the governess's mind Quint is a character to be read. Likewise, her entire history at Bly is a letter to be read. She wants to read it right. She has tried twice before and apparently is not content with her success. Her written narrative is a third attempt to read the truth.

Implicit in these multiple attempts is the impossibility of reading and articulating the true meaning of experience. Absolute truth needs an objective support, the guarantee of unimpeachable authority. The governess may desire to read the true meaning of Miles's death, but without superhuman authority, she can never articulate an unequivocal interpretation. So she searches for a master reader.

Her desires to tell the truth and for Douglas's sympathetic attention suggest that what she wants from Douglas is confirmation of her reading. She has told him the story, and he seems to have asked questions. She retells him the story, perhaps slightly readjusted. Her whole motive may be described as, "Have I got it right this time?" This motive, if it is correct, seems extraordinarily important. She trusts him deeply. She is willing to give him the whole story as she knows it, without conscious omissions, including even more probing self-criticism than we have yet seen. What she wants is that he mirror her, not necessarily as she sees herself from within, but as she really is, as a whole person. As Brooke-Rose has argued, she wants an objective, authoritative portrait of herself.[12] This, of course, is also what we want, for only in such a portrait can we hope to find an answer to the question of whether she saved Miles.

The governess trustfully requests a loving judgment from Douglas. She says to him in effect: "Read me and, because you love me, tell me the whole truth of what you see. To help you and because I love and trust you, I will tell you all that I see of myself." If as we may well suspect, the governess is as difficult to read as are Quint and the whole affair at Bly, then what she asks is impossible. And, as we saw in the prologue, just this impossibility keeps the chain of communications extending itself toward the fictional master reader.

Just as the governess's presentation of herself as a reader at Bly both inspires and qualifies our confidence in her ability to read experience at twenty, so her self-presentation as a woman past thirty looking back on her youth does the same. She emerges as quite extraordinary in her narration, because there she shows herself as sharing our rereading project. She has had our thoughts and has reread before us. By greatly complicating the problem of evaluating her judgments, this discovery moves her closer to intellectual and moral equality with the reader. Even though she opens herself in this private communication as she would only to a beloved, she possesses depths of character that neither she nor we are likely to plumb. At the same time that her authority is enhanced by a fuller revelation of her capacities, the value of any interpretive authority short of a god's is undercut when we remember that this is her third version.

"He did stand there!—but high up, beyond the lawn and at the very top of the tower" (10).

Illustration by Eric Pape, from *Collier's Weekly* 20, no. 19 (12 February 1898):21. Courtesy of the New York State Historical Association Library.

7

A Bewilderment of Vision:
The Governess and the Ghosts

When the governess compares Quint to the letters she is forming on her page, she calls attention to the necessity of reading him. As a result of the appearance of ghosts, she soon finds it necessary as well to read the children. The authority with which she reads them all is of considerable importance to our attempt to read her. Like readers before us, we need to know whether the ghosts she sees are really present or only projected by her and, if they are there, whether she accurately assesses the ghosts' intentions.

QUEER COMPANY: THE REALITY OF THE GHOSTS

There are good reasons for believing the ghosts are real. The crucial appearances for establishing their reality or lack of it are the first three. After Quint has appeared twice, the governess and Mrs. Grose identify him. Miss Jessel is identified after her first appearance.

The governess recounts describing Quint to Mrs. Grose in considerable detail, and Mrs. Grose asks several questions to verify her hypothesis before pronouncing Quint's name. During this episode, the governess believes she is describing a living man rather than an apparition. Only after Mrs. Grose has named him does she inform the governess that he is dead and, therefore, a ghost. The governess records her surprise at learning this news: " 'Died?' I almost shrieked" (24). This conversation is followed by others she does not record: "We had gone over and over every feature of what I had seen" (25).

The account the governess gives of her first discussion with Mrs. Grose of Jessel's appearance is equivocal, for the governess assumes before the conversation begins that she has seen Jessel's ghost. The physical portrait is less detailed, with more attention to moral qualities, the interpretation of Jessel's intentions. This description, nevertheless, makes it past Mrs. Grose's challenging skepticism: "Tell me how you know" (32). As with the identification of Quint, there follow more unreported conversations in which the governess could well have supplied enough data to make good her assertion that she could not have made up her visions, for she had created "a portrait on the exhibition of which she [Mrs. Grose] had instantly recognised and named them" (34).

The persuasiveness and sincerity of the governess's testimony do not give it authority, however. We can undercut her authority simply by pointing out alternate sources of information about Quint and Jessel. Freudian readers have emphasized the importance of the governess's inquiries, perhaps even in the village, about Quint's first appearance. There it would have been possible, in conversation, to learn about Quint and Jessel. She asserts that she heard no breath of scandal about Bly (26), but she also indicates that, according to Mrs. Grose, the inquest into Quint's death left unanswered questions in the community (28). So, although the Quint and Jessel sexual affair was not known in the village, Quint was certainly rather well known. It becomes possible, at least, that the governess could have learned enough about him to present him to Mrs. Grose convincingly. Though we have no textual evidence of where she might have obtained an equally detailed description of Jessel, once we have identified the village as a source for Quint, we may not go too far by letting it or the other servants at Bly be sources for information about Jessel.

The point of this reaching out to the borders of what her text will allow is to show that the slightest suggestion that the governess had access to details about Quint and Jessel makes possible her hallucinations. She really saw them. She persuasively described them to Mrs. Grose. But, her unconscious grasped details she picked up in the village or among the servants and presented them to her as these apparitions. Her unconscious read in Mrs. Grose's slip about the man who used to like women young and pretty the former presence of a now deceased, sexually predatory male. Without her conscious knowledge, her unconscious can have found the characters necessary to manifest its desire to her consciousness. This would require considerable forgetting on the part of a woman who seems extraordinarily self-aware, but the unconscious has proven more than capable of such feats. I am willing to accept the possibility that she obtained information about which she has forgotten mainly because doing so makes little difference to the meaning of the tale. James left open only a very small ambiguity in her testimony about what she sees. I am inclined to believe that he intended readers to believe that she saw actual apparitions of Quint and Jessel, but I cannot prove even this; I can only make the ghosts' reality seem probable. How much more problematic is her interpretation of what she sees!

While it is not perfectly certain that what she sees is really there, we have small room to doubt that the governess tells the truth. In this, her second account, she remains convinced. Whether or not ghosts appear, she almost certainly sees what she comes to believe are the ghosts of Quint and Jessel. It is hard to overemphasize that even if these apparitions arise from her unconscious, they are as real to her consciousness as if they had truly come from infernal regions. For her and for us, the issue is not whether she saw anything, but whether what she saw was real. Though they may have been real, we cannot find textual evidence to prove this. If the ghosts are unreal, then Flora and Miles may suffer needlessly. But even if they are real, the children's fate depends upon how the governess reads what she sees.

A KIND OF FURY OF INTENTION: WHAT THE GHOSTS WANT

The governess's interpretation of the ghosts' intentions moves through phases as the manifestations multiply. Quint is at first a strange intruder come without permission to survey the landscape from atop the old tower. Upon his second visit the governess detects his intention to see and be seen by Miles (26). When the governess guesses this intention, she learns from Mrs. Grose that Quint has a history of showing too much interest in Miles, of wishing to spoil him, of being "too free" with him and with everyone (26). The governess's response to this conclusion is that she will sacrifice herself to protect the children, that she will offer herself as the "sole subject" of such visions in order to "fence about and absolutely save" the children (26). For a number of reasons, this strategy is naive. How can she know she is protecting them? By what means can she offer herself as sole visionary? Her use of the term *fence about* recalls her previous naive fancy that her job might be to preserve the children from adulthood (15).

The governess seems to be aware that this response was probably inadequate. It was never tested, so she cannot be perfectly sure it was the wrong response, but she speaks of it with some irony. As she writes her account she remains proud that she saw her response "strongly and simply" as to protect the helpless children, but she also implies that this response was mad. Because she could not be sure at any time that her seeing prevented the children seeing, she watched them with a "disguised tension" that might easily have become madness had not the situation been redefined by the appearance of Jessel (28).

Jessel's first visit forces the governess to revise her reading of the ghosts' intentions. She concludes that both children see both ghosts and want to conceal their communication. Mrs. Grose, always unwilling to gossip, now admits that Quint and Jessel were lovers, despite the difference in their rank. Taken together, this speculation and information elicit the conclusion that the children are lost. They are already in communication with the ghosts, and the governess cannot shield and absolutely save them.

A Bewilderment of Vision: The Governess and the Ghosts

The governess is confirmed in this conclusion when she learns more from Mrs. Grose about Quint and Jessel's relations with the children. Mrs. Grose suspects, but is unwilling to believe, that the pair used the children in such a way that the youngsters could hardly fail to understand the sexual nature of their relationship. Miles may even have helped conceal "their relation" (37).

Despite her being so sure, the governess reserves judgment, refusing to accuse either child of carrying on a concealed intercourse with evil spirits. Her main reason for refusing to accept her own conclusion is that she has seen no evidence of corruption in the children. Subsequent events turn her attention to a closer scrutiny of the children's moral state. This turn is the subject of the next chapter.

In the ghosts the governess sees absolutely evil intentions. She believes they want to possess and destroy the children, without regard for their innocence or goodness. By almost any civilized standard, such a desire approaches absolute evil. Mrs. Grose also comes to believe in the reality and the absolute evil of the ghosts. They have violated central taboos, fornicating across class lines, and they have involved children in their crimes. Stating the lovers' sins in this way considerably diminishes the absoluteness of their evil, raising the question of whether the governess reads her fears, conscious and unconscious, into the ghosts. For James in 1897, when he composed the tale, the misdeeds of Quint and Jessel would also have seemed considerably less serious than they are for the governess and Mrs. Grose.

Contemporary readers apparently imagined much worse. For example, Peter Beidler cites the contemporary interpretation of W. H. Myers, one of James's acquaintances, given in a private letter. Myers believed that Miles feels "pederastic passion" for Quint's ghost, that Flora feels "lesbian love" for Jessel's ghost, that Jessel committed suicide while pregnant, and that the bisexual Quint was murdered by one of his male victims.[13] In this interpretation, Quint, Jessel, and the children have been bad indeed by the standards of their society. James saw Oscar Wilde sentenced to hard labor for admitting sodomy. Yet James and many of his intellectual and artistic contemporaries felt sorry for Wilde. They saw him less as the great sinner than as a victim of a society that condemned not the behavior itself so much as the public admission. In short, James and many of his associates would not have seen evil worthy of damnation in the sins, reported and guessed, of Quint and Jessel.

That the governess sees absolute evil in the ghosts following naturally from their sins in life shows her to be unaware of the undercurrents of her society. She may also be unaware of her personal secrets, of the motions of her unconscious. Seeing them embodied, she may distance herself from the embodiments by insisting too much upon their corruption.

Both the governess and Mrs. Grose tend on occasion to moderate their condemnations. Both express pity for Jessel, though never for Quint. It is in the governess's interest, after all, to keep open her conscious dream of earning the uncle's notice and admiration. Implicitly, she entertains hope of a sexual relationship, legitimized by marriage of course, across class boundaries similar to those dividing Quint and Jessel. The distance between Quint and Jessel's fate and deservings, as well as the governess's pity for Jessel, tend to suggest that she interprets the ghosts' intentions out of her needs rather than merely by inferring from their behavior.

PERHAPS SHE LIKES IT: ALTERNATE GHOSTS

When the governess tells Mrs. Grose that Flora communicates with Jessel, Mrs. Grose responds, "Perhaps she likes it! . . . Is n't it just a proof of her blest innocence?" (32). Though the governess characterizes these remarks as a grim joke, they offer a hint of alternate ways of reading these visions. Perhaps Flora's innocence protects her from the ghosts, or perhaps the ghosts only appear evil to the governess and not to the children. Of course, the main alternate way of reading them that criticism has given us is that the governess reads into the ghosts meanings from her own unconscious, that, in fact, all the unusual manifestations and their interpretations originate in the governess's unconscious. But there are other possibilities.

For example, what if we consider Mrs. Grose's remarks about the children's possible pleasure in meeting with the ghosts in the context of their extraordinarily angelic behavior and in relation to our perception that Quint and Jessel, though violators of social taboo, were not absolutely evil in life? Perhaps Quint and Jessel, like some of the more romantic ghosts of the past, have returned to the scene of their guilt and joy. In this case, the children may or may not be aware of their presence. If the children are aware, they may be participating as they did before, in ways that have not obviously or certainly affected their moral life. Or the children may be involved in ways quite different. Quint and Jessel were the third pair of parental figures the children lost. It is possible that while the ghosts have come for each other, the children are using the poor spirits for their own different reasons. Yet another alternative is argued by E. W. Sheppard who says the governess may be telepathically sensitive to the evil planted in the children by the lovers. She resolves this sensitivity into apparitions she thinks are ghosts and, as a result, magnifies relative vice into absolute metaphysical evil.[14]

If the ghosts are like texts, then anyone can read them in whatever way seems suitable. If they are silent texts, then one is likely to read oneself into them. This, of course, is what many critics suspect the governess has done. The governess herself is worried about this possibility, as will be clearer when we discuss her relations with the children. Why should we challenge her reading of the ghosts?

One of the problems with her visions is that no rule governs them. According to her interpretation of the ghosts' intentions, they may well have been present and in communication with the children for about a year, yet the governess begins seeing spirits not upon her arrival, but at a particular point in her stay. Likewise, she temporarily ceases seeing them and begins seeing them again. While it was commonly believed in 1897 that ghostly appearances often seem arbitrary, this did not mean they were not rule-governed. Indeed, one purpose of psychical research was to uncover laws that might determine the conditions of spirit manifestations. Looking at a list of the apparitions may help to find a rule governing the changes in her relations to the ghosts.

Apparitions of the Ghosts

June and into the summer:

1. Quint at twilight on the old tower.
2. Quint on Sunday after tea outside the dining room window.
3. Jessel in the afternoon by the lake, Flora present.
4. Quint at midnight on the stair.
5. Jessel at midnight at the bottom of the stair.

November, after a long interruption in appearances:

6. Jessel in the schoolroom, Sunday morning.
7. Jessel by the lake, Flora and Mrs. Grose present.
8. Quint after lunch outside the dining room window, Miles present.

Critics have examined these events closely for patterns that would suggest some rule for their occurrence. Many patterns are apparent, most notably the patterns of symmetry that Brooke-Rose points out.[15] The spirits never appear together; Jessel is never seen in Miles's presence, and Quint never in Flora's. Each spirit appears four times, twice inside the house, and twice outside. Quint is three times below the governess and once above her, while she sees Jessel three times on her own level—one of these in her own place at the schoolroom table—and once below her. She meets each up close just once and sees them at a distance or with a barrier between them each of the other three times. The governess exchanges positions with each ghost once, taking Quint's place outside the window after his second appearance and taking Jessel's position at the bottom of the stair just before her third appearance. Patterns of relative movement can be traced through these and other symmetries, and Brooke-Rose has done so in a way that suggests that the governess rather than laws governing ghosts determines these patterns.

Surface differences between the apparitions also seem to point at the governess as much as at the ghosts determining their visibility. The governess describes Quint's appearances as confrontational, as contests over rights, territory, the children. Jessel only once looks at and directly communicates with the governess; instead, her objects seem more directly the children. The governess sees a danger that Jessel will draw Flora away and thereby replace the governess. While this consistency suggests gender differentiation of the ghosts' behavior, it also reflects the governess's differing attitudes toward the two.

If we look more closely at the occasions upon which the ghosts turn up, we have only the governess's situation to consider. If there are patterns in the occasions, we are almost certain to read these as products of the governess. When we examine the first appearance of each, we discover interesting similarities. Each is preceded by the governess going through a phase of self-praise that includes a revealing wish.

In June the governess was caught up in the spell of her pleasant work. After the children are put to bed, there remains ample light for an evening walk. She uses "her hour" to imagine a story in which during her walk she would meet the uncle, who would stand before her "and smile and approve" (15). She is in this fantasy when she sees Quint and thinks at first that he is the master. This is the only time he appears to her in the master's position, on the tower from which he commands a view. She reflects that this is not where she had imagined seeing him; rather than above her, she has been imagining him on her level. His not being in the "right" place leads to her discovering that she does not recognize him, and for a moment, she sees two figures simultaneously, or so she seems to mean when she says she suffers "a bewilderment of vision" that she cannot adequately convey (16).

She wishes to see the uncle on the path, praising her. Instead, he appears on the tower, and before her eyes is transformed from the approving uncle into a sinister figure who exhibits a "strange freedom" toward her and who fixes her with the same question "that his own presence provoked" (17). Presumably this question is "What are you doing here?"

If we read this incident wondering why the governess would see what she sees in whatever may be there, the pattern of her experience suggests at least one possible answer. She is allowing herself to indulge in fantasies. In fact, she has not done a good job, for she is ignoring the problem of Miles's school. She only pretends that she deserves the master's praise and that his approval is all she wants, for she also wants to remove the social barrier between them, to bring him down to her level, where further social relations can become possible. The governess says she is not afraid to confess her fantasies. This suggests that she has come to understand her attitude toward the master as well as she understands her failure to consider Miles's future. But she shows no clear awareness, as she composes, of her probable desire to achieve social equality with the uncle and of what this suggests about her unconscious. She never moves beyond saying that she would have liked him to know and appreciate her efforts.

Quint appears, in this reading, as a recognition of reality, asserting that the master is above her and challenging her right to be at Bly. For this reason her imagination may transform him into a dark double of the master, a sexually dangerous man dressed in the master's clothes. This transformation may reveal another aspect of her unconscious desire, the desire for sexual union with the master that she has kept out of her consciousness. Her desire would appear transformed as external, belonging to the man, and evil, forbidden to her. In this reading, he is also a double of her.

In the days before Jessel's first appearance, the governess is again indulging in fantasies. Then she sees herself as the heroine who will be a shield between children and ghosts to save the youngsters absolutely. She dreams of the "greatness of letting it be seen . . . in the right quarter" (28). We have seen that these are naive fantasies. When she sees Jessel, the governess is with Flora by the lake, where both are pretending that the governess is "something very important and quiet" (29). The governess is stitching as she sits on her bench, when she becomes aware of a presence. She apparently assumes that Quint is watching them; at least, all of the identities she imagines are male. She refuses to look at the figure until she has gathered her courage and studied Flora's reaction. Flora's response is to become silent, but also to continue playing intently: "She had picked up a small flat piece of wood which happened to have in it a little hole that had evidently suggested to her the idea of sticking in another fragment that might figure as a mast and make the thing a boat. This second morsel . . . she was very markedly and intently attempting to tighten in its place"

(30). When the governess finally looks up, she discovers Jessel rather than Quint, and almost immediately divines that Quint and Jessel have been lovers and that the children commune with the ghosts, as she reveals to Mrs. Grose two hours later.

Like Quint, Jessel first turns up in the context of the governess thinking too well of herself and wishing for the impossible. That the governess is required by the rules of the current game to be important and quiet reminds us of the injunction of silent responsibility under which she works. It also suggests that she is in a position to "listen" to her unconscious. Both she and Flora, it turns out, are engaged in suggestive activity, moving small "morsels" through holes, but Flora's more strongly suggests a sexual analogy. This does not necessarily mean that Flora is consciously playing sexual games; rather, the governess has before her at the moment of vision a sexually significant image. And she presents this image in interesting words.

The governess's reading of Flora's activity suggests a symbolic crossing of the barrier between where they sit and where the governess believes a spectral man waits. The mast gives the boat access to the power of the wind, making it whole and free, an image of the governess's desire. The mast must be screwed into the boat for this to work, in the way she and the master must be united if her wish is to be fulfilled. The mast is a morsel, connoting that she may see it as like food. Meanings such as this are available to the governess's unconscious before she looks upon this apparition.

That she sees a fallen woman seems almost natural, if we are looking for reasons she might identify whatever she sees as Jessel. It appears the governess expected Quint and got Jessel, as before she expected the uncle and got Quint. Likewise, looking on images of her unconscious desire before looking up leads her to see a critique that is also the image of desire. Jessel shows her what she might really become were she to attract the master's interest. She consciously rejects this, but her unconscious does not care about morality; it wants sexual union with the uncle on any terms.

While we can no more prove this reading accurate than we could that of Quint's debut, that they are consistent with each other gives them authority. Once we have seen this or some similar meaning in these events, it is fairly easy to read the other apparitions in a similar way.

The second time she sees Quint, she remarks that "it was as if I had been looking at him for years and had known him always" (20). His face, seen up close for the first time, is as familiar to her as if she had always known it, as if she had become obsessed with it. When she goes out to investigate, she does something rather strange: "It was confusedly present to me that I ought to place myself where he had stood. . . . As if, at this moment, to show me exactly what his range had been, Mrs. Grose . . . came in from the hall" (21). What leads her to take Quint's perspective? What are we to make of the subsequent reenactment of the scare with the governess standing in for Quint and Mrs. Grose standing in for the governess? Does the governess reveal the Quint in herself by her familiarity with him and by her taking his perspective? Is the repetition James's way of underlining this hint? The details here seem insufficient to create much certainty, but as in each apparition we find incongruous details calling our attention to a deeper, hidden layer of meaning that the governess fails to see, but that we might glimpse.

One of the purposes of this examination of alternate readings of the ghosts is to flesh out some of the details of a Freudian reading and to show that neither the Freudian reading nor the governess's can lay claim to absolute authority. Another purpose will become clear as we look more closely at the middle pair of visitations. Most critics who psychoanalyze the governess create fairly persuasive readings of the supernatural events not unlike those above. But, accounting psychoanalytically for her ceasing for so long to see the ghosts is more of a problem. Brooke-Rose notes that the apparitions stop after Mrs. Grose "threatens" to write to the uncle and the governess says she will leave if this happens, and the apparitions begin again after Miles threatens to call in the uncle. Brooke-Rose believes the governess understands that she would be unable to retain her perspective under the critique of the uncle. For this reason she transfers her visions to the children.[16] That Mrs. Grose's threat causes appearances to cease temporarily is difficult to prove. Mrs. Grose makes her suggestion after Miles's trick, which takes place at least several days after the last apparition, and it seems clear that the fourth and fifth apparitions are different in that the governess sees herself as above and as stronger than the ghosts. These last two meetings of the summer hint at other reasons for the change.

In her third meeting with Quint the governess seems to banish him from the house. Having by this point conceived of her mission as a struggle with the ghosts over possession of the children, her courage has become less foolish. She depends on her sensitivity to the ghosts to fend them off, watching the children continuously by day and patrolling the house when her intuition draws her out in the night. On the night in question, as she leaves her room, she again thinks about her desire to be seen by the uncle (40). In the meeting with Quint that follows, there is mutual recognition: "He knew me as well as I knew him" (41). She finds that though she loathes him, she is no longer afraid of him. Presumably, this courage comes from her love for the children. She describes their confrontation as unnaturally horrifying in its dead silence: "The moment was so prolonged that it would have taken but little more to make me doubt if even *I* were in life" (41). The threat of this silence is that it might absorb her, that she might become like Quint, one of the silent dead. But she is stronger, for she banishes him around the next bend of the stair into silence and darkness: "I definitely saw it turn, as I might have seen the low wretch to which it had once belonged turn on receipt of an order" (41). She never sees him again inside the house.

As before, she wishes to see and be seen by the master, but sees and is seen by Quint instead. This time, however, she asserts her mastery over Quint. She came to Bly as the master's representative. Now she will act the part, banishing the master's false double. She has taken hold of the helm at which she found herself on her first day. Beneath this, it is hinted, is self-recognition. If Quint stands for her unconscious desire for sexual union with the master, she seems to assert control over that desire by facing it and then reenacting its repression. If this is true, then it follows that her next vision should be of Jessel, alone in pain at the bottom of the stair. If Jessel represents the governess's sexual desire freed of moral restraint, then this vision shows that desire defeated and, perhaps, tamed. It also follows that the governess would not see the ghosts again unless she finds further use for them. She has asserted the authority delegated to her to be the master for the uncle.

The word *turn* is repeated here, and it reminds us that the stairway turns back on itself, that it is in the shape of a screw. Metaphorically, in the governess's act of banishing, the top of the stairs is the territory of consciousness and innocence, where she and the children sleep. She guards this area most vigorously. The bottom of the stairs is the territory of darkness and silence, of the unconscious. By issuing her metaphorical order, she turns the screw, spiraling the ghosts down the stairs into the unconscious from which they have attempted to escape. That they become invisible until new circumstances bring them back indicates that for the time being the governess has gained control over her unconscious desires.

We have begun a deeper analysis of the governess. Perhaps, here near the outset it would be well to examine a little more closely the reasons for and methods of such an analysis. It should be clear that the impulse to analyze the governess arises from James's stimulation of our skepticism. James's audience was perhaps only a little more inclined than we to believe that outside of fiction the dead return as ghosts. Upon first reading, this tale seems to be such a fiction. But rereading follows from our doubts about the governess's interpretations and confronts us more absolutely with her uniqueness. That she alone sees the ghosts licenses and demands our search for alternative explanations.

The history of this search has been odd in several ways that make our present task more difficult. Psychoanalyses have tended to focus on the governess and to ignore the children, and they have tended to overstate the case. The governess has often been painted as violently psychotic and uniquely diseased, while the children are generally seen as completely free of abnormality. A systematic attempt to explain why psychoanalytic readings have taken this path would make an interesting book. We might ask why mainly male readers choose the woman as the villain or why the Freudian vision of dark childhood fantasies is rarely applied in this case. My analyses, which follow in subsequent chapters, tend to show the governess as closer to normality than has often been argued, and they attend to unconscious desires in the children as well as the governess. We have already seen that the ghosts, if they are real, may have their own point of view, independent of the governess's interpretations.

How are we readers to psychoanalyze a character? We know that professional analysts undergo years of rigorous training and receive official licenses to practice. What licenses have we? There are at least two available to us. These do not guarantee our expertise, but they do justify our attempt. The first general license comes from our experiences of reading literature and living in society. The second specific license comes from James himself.

We daily study each other, making guesses about incompletely expressed meanings and hidden motives. A coffee or study break at any institution will offer numerous examples. Readers of literature and viewers of drama hone their skills by analyzing the fictional characters they meet. In most of modern literature, we find authors creating characters with unconscious, hidden sides. Fundamental to understanding such characters are concepts any sophisticated reader has mastered to some degree: disguising one's desires in ways that open one to unconscious motives, attributing one's unconscious motives to others, dealing through kinds of personification and other symbols with unknown but powerful inner forces, directing the energy of a forbidden desire toward a socially approved activity. These concepts were all given technical names by Freud: repression, projection, dream work, and sublimation. Any reader of Shakespeare, Jane Austen, Melville, or Hawthorne could intuit and observe such activities. All experienced readers have a general license and the basic skills to look beneath the surface of the governess's narrative for what she may not know about herself.

James gives us permission to psychoanalyze the governess by rewarding us for the effort. As soon as we are made to doubt her, at least by the end of the first reading, we must focus on her character. As soon as we see in the prologue that she is caught up in patterns of repetition and mirroring, we may suspect that unconscious motives have entered into her seeing and interpreting. Our skepticism about the reality of ghosts leads quite naturally to our wondering why she would imagine them. And, as we have seen in our look at the first apparitions, when we ask why she might imagine them, we find suggestions of a pattern of unconscious motivation. When we look for a rule that might explain why they begin to appear when they do, we find possible causes in the governess. We can see ways in which the apparitions connect with needs it seems reasonable to attribute to her. James has anticipated our deeper analysis of the governess.

While these two licenses grant permission and affirm our general skills, they do not give us expertise. Part of my job as a professional reader is to bring to bear on this story some information about psychoanalysis. This knowledge, however, has severe limits, for I have not undergone training as an analyst. I can bring only an interested layman's understanding of psychoanalytic concepts to our reading. For this reason, my interpretations of the governess are determined more by what she says and does than by my knowledge of psychoanalytic theory. While this is an important limitation on my readings, it may also be an advantage, for it helps to keep me aware of another limitation that may elude both the novice psychoanalyzer and the professional. There is an absolutely crucial limit to psychoanalysis that we must carefully observe from the beginning of our plunge into the governess's depths.

How can we know when we have accurately interpreted the governess's unconscious motives? Since I find most previous psychoanalytic readings inadequate, I have tried to provide better readings in this study. They are, I believe, more comprehensive and account more fully and more appropriately for the details presented in the governess's narrative. Their authority comes from internal consistency and from their correspondence to the text. Notice, however, that as with the governess's account, there is no external authority to support my analysis, no matter how much superiority I am able to establish for it.

A Bewilderment of Vision: The Governess and the Ghosts

Where would such authority come from? Perhaps, were I influential enough, I could persuade an organization of psychoanalysts to express an opinion on my analysis. If they validated my conclusions, would we then know the truth about the governess? I am afraid not. Though psychoanalysts have been known to claim that they have fully and accurately interpreted cases in which the subject died before undergoing analysis or was a fictional character, contemporary theory, such as that offered by Jacques Lacan, would undercut any such claim.

Lacan and his followers would argue that every individual's unconscious really is unique, even though it shares patterns of development with the unconsciouses of most other people of the same culture and sex. Therefore, I cannot specify with confidence the workings of any individual's unconscious. The only possible source of authority for my reading of what another does not say directly is the person who speaks. Could the governess appear to us now, listen to and fully comprehend our analysis, and without coercion of any kind—a very subtle problem when one is revealing her unknown thoughts to her—affirm our interpretation, then we might with confidence believe we are right. In the absence of this sort of confirmation, we stand toward the governess just as she stands toward the ghosts. We read her secrets on our authority alone. We can talk with each other as she talks with Mrs. Grose, and so agree on what we think. We can go, as she cannot, to trained experts, who may well correct and modify our ideas, producing a new agreement with professional authority supporting it. These do not give us the truth, only strong agreement on what we think the truth might be. The fact remains that the truth is hidden, and we can only guess at it. The best guess is still a guess.

Keeping this in mind, we turn to the relations between the governess and the children.

"Holding my candle high, till I came within sight of the tall window" (40).
Illustration by Eric Pape, from *Collier's Weekly* 20, no. 22 (5 March 1898):17.
Courtesy of the New York State Historical Association Library.

8

The Strangeness of Our Fate:
The Governess and the Children

Infernal Imagination:
The Governess Reads the Children

In June, when the governess first meets Flora, she believes she sees the perfection of childhood. Miles makes such an impression upon her that she dismisses the implied warning of the letter from the headmaster. By early autumn she is convinced that the children are possessed by evil spirits, even though Mrs. Grose is unable to see any outward sign of their inner danger. This shift in the governess's point of view is crucial, for it leads to confrontations with the children that issue in Flora's illness and Miles's death. Though we have been unable to accord the governess absolute authority in her reading of the ghosts, perhaps we can find the help we need by examining her relations with the children.

It is useful to notice that she records eight crisis points in dealing with the children and to list them in relation to the ghostly apparitions.

The Apparitions and Crises with the Children

Quint on old tower	
Quint outside window (1)	
Jessel by lake (1)	Flora sees Jessel (?)
Quint on stair	Flora at window (1)
Jessel on stair	
	Flora at window (2)
	Miles goes outside (trick)
	Miles wants freedom
Jessel in schoolroom	
	In Miles's room
	Flora goes outside (trick)
Jessel by lake (2)	
Quint outside window (2)	Miles dies.

As with the apparitions, we can discover many interesting patterns and symmetries in this list, but our main concern for now is the shift in the governess's attention from the ghosts through Flora to Miles that is reflected in the first six crises. The shift is completed when Miles plays his trick, arranging for the governess to discover him on the lawn at midnight. This is followed by two conversations between the governess and Miles, and these eventuate in the governess determining that she must take action.

In the first crucial conversation with Miles, the governess detects a plan. He explains that it is past time for him to return to school and that he wishes to go. As they discuss this matter, the governess thinks she sees a deeper idea.

From Miles's demonstration of badness—the first trick—the children learned that the governess is afraid of something. This is clearest in her decision to seek a point of view from which she can see what Flora sees without confronting Flora directly. How else would they explain her finding another window from which to view the lawn rather than joining Flora at her window? With the prank Miles asserts power and independence, while also discovering or verifying her weakness. He says to her, "Think, you know, what I *might* do!" (48). The governess believes this shows Miles fully aware of the distinction between good and evil and of the degree to which he has been good. Implicitly this statement is a threat, an assertion of power for an as yet unstated purpose. When he asks about school, Miles reveals his reason. Then she sees that he wants to use her fear of trying to explain "this queer business of ours" to increase his freedom (62). To her, this means that Miles wants more freedom to associate with Quint. If she will not cooperate, then he will arrange for the uncle to come straighten matters out, perhaps leading to her dismissal.

As a result of this conversation and of consultation with Mrs. Grose, the governess decides that she will have to write to the uncle. To give in to Miles is certainly to lose him, while involving the uncle may keep the situation open a little longer. Before actually writing the letter, she tries once more to talk with Miles. She asks him to confide in her, reminding him that if the uncle comes, Miles will have to explain his behavior. He repeats that he wants only to be left alone. She cannot accept this answer, for to her it means what she cannot bear, the repetition of Miles being sent home from school. For the first time she directly approaches the forbidden subject of the past: "What happened before?" (64). She detects in his response a hint that he might truly confess: "it made me drop on my knees beside the bed and seize once more the chance of possessing him" (65). When she says she wants Miles to help her save him, she experiences a supernatural blast and chill that shake the room and put out her candle. She hears Miles shriek, but does not know if the note is of jubilation or terror. Yet in the next instant the room seems undisturbed, and Miles calmly announces that he has blown out her candle.

The governess's reticence here is troubling, for she never attempts to explain her two contradictory impressions in this interview. The key points that emerge from Miles's trick and these two conversations, however, are that the children are apparently cooperating to escape her comprehensive supervision, but that Miles may also want to escape the ghosts.

The governess concludes that the children are possessed by evil spirits and that she can save them. She is acutely aware that her reading is completely subjective and that it seems mad. She has seen the children begin to behave strangely. Why are they suddenly so interested in what happens outside the house at night? As Eli Siegel has argued, she has seen that they conspire, that they have a life apart from her, and that in their private life, she is manipulable.[17] They have shown her a power of independent action. These signs confirm what the letter from the headmaster implied, that there is a secret, invisible side to these children. This aspect is present to the governess in their silence about their past. She reminds Mrs. Grose that they have never spoken about their past to her at all, about Quint, Jessel, or Miles's school. The revelation of their secret side casts light back upon her previous impression, on the true unnaturalness of their beauty and goodness. Young children really never are so good. By their behavior the children invite the governess's reading, and by their silence they invite her conclusion that they are possessed. Miles's prank unites her observations in a single revealing instance. And his demand for freedom gives meaning to all the manifestations; this is where all the strange events have been heading, the final corruption and deaths of the children.

Her conclusion about the children's state remains provisional, however, until Miles demands greater freedom. Then, whether she is certain or not, she must act. She writes to the uncle. In fact, she is not certain. She asserts that during the month between Miles's prank and his demand their relations with the ghosts were clear to her: "It was not, I am as sure to-day as I was sure then, my mere infernal imagination: it was absolutely traceable that they were aware of my predicament and that this strange relation made, in a manner, for a long time, the air in which we moved" (50). Her assertion alone shows she is aware as she writes that an outside observer would consider her overly imaginative. She was aware at the time, as well, that she would be unable to convince another with the evidence in hand. This was her main reason for being unwilling to involve the master. Were a skeptical authority called in, he or she would surely conclude that the children are innocent and the governess mad. The effect of this conclusion would be, if the governess is not mad, to condemn the children to destruction by the ghosts.

As the governess explains her evidence to Douglas, it becomes clear why it would not convince a skeptical observer. It is completely subjective, consisting almost exclusively of silences and odd but inconclusive behavior. Though the governess is absolutely convinced by the cumulative intensity of her subjective experiences that the children communicate with the ghosts even in her presence, she is tragically trapped in that subjectivity. Not even the sympathetic Mrs. Grose can share it, and Mrs. Grose declines to believe the children in serious danger as long as there are no palpable signs. The governess is called upon to act without verification from an external authority.

She must either deny her subjective impressions and leave the children to whatever their fate may be, or she must try to regain possession of them herself. The latter alternative means getting them to freely acknowledge their relations with the ghosts and then, knowing what they do and why, end those relations. To do this, she must talk with them about the ghosts. When Flora stands at the window the first time, the governess wishes she could say: "You see, you see, you *know* that you do and that you already quite suspect I believe it; therefore why not frankly confess it to me, so that we may at least live with it together and learn perhaps, in the strangeness of our fate, where we are and what it means?" (42). This, however, is forbidden by social convention and by the children as well, for they are silent.

It is important to realize the absoluteness of the command that she not speak to the children about these ghosts. The source of this injunction is her education and background as a Victorian. She feels entrapped more than once by "the old tradition of the criminality of those caretakers of the young who minister to superstitions and fears" (47). In this society the moral innocence of children is presumed, and an adult's responsibility is to preserve it. The governess is silenced in part because to speak of Quint and Jessel means to advert to their sexual irregularities, thus violating a particularly important facet of childhood innocence. She is also silenced by the skepticism of her society. Ghosts, after all, are not real; to treat them as real before children is to encourage unhealthy superstition.

The governess sees these problems perhaps a little more deeply than her society, for she understands that by giving names to the forbidden, she opens it to the imagination. By speaking to them of the dead she might help the children "to represent something infamous" (53). This injunction, like the master's, is also a double bind for the governess. If she remains silent and the children are lost, she is responsible for harming them. If she speaks to and thus corrupts innocent children, she harms them directly. The only way she can win is to be sure of her reading, but she can never be sure. In the face of this uncertainty, she chooses to act positively according to her subjective impressions. She loves the children; therefore, she will try to save them.

FINE MACHINERY: READING THE GOVERNESS

Because the governess's case for believing the children possessed is tenuously grounded in her subjective experience, it is little wonder that skeptical readers have done just what she expected the master would do. She tells Mrs. Grose that to reveal the haunting of the children would be to expose herself as having invented "fine machinery" to attract the uncle's notice to her "slighted charms" (50). One of the ironies of her reading of the children is that her most impressive demonstrations of acuity coincide with her most tenuous observations and conclusions. The delicacy and sensitivity of her observations are clear, yet what she sees undercuts our impression of those very qualities. What happens to fineness of perception and judgment in the service of serious error?

We should not forget that in reading the children as she does, the governess responds to objective events. The children cannot be hallucinations without our radically altering basic assumptions about this story. The reality of the children as opposed to the ghosts does not release us from the governess's subjectivity, for she is the only witness of most of their odd behavior. Mrs. Grose sees but does not read the letter from the headmaster. She sees some aftereffects in the children of Miles's request for freedom, when they agree not to mention the governess's missing church. She sees Flora's final escapade and its consequences. Nevertheless, all the most important perceptions are the governess's alone.

If we continue to grant that the children really do what she sees and hears them doing, then their behavior is provocative. Their cooperation in Miles's trick shows them to be precociously artful and secretive. They have carefully worked out her probable reactions. Staying awake without revealing themselves and coordinating their actions while apart shows them much more capable than ordinary children their age. We can also see that when the governess's attention shifts from ghosts to children, she gives up her power to unconsciously manipulate what she sees.

Flora's apparently spontaneous act of arising from bed on the same night the governess banishes Quint seems to preclude the governess unconsciously controlling the children's movements. Indeed, for the period in which the ghosts are invisible to the governess, the children seem to direct her seeing as they wish. Psychoanalytic readers have argued that the children are disturbed by her odd behavior, especially the intensity of attention she gives to them. This may be true, but their disturbance leads not so much to recognizable symptoms of stress as to the appearance of a studied investigation of the governess by the children.

A pattern that emerges from the chart of crises suggests that the children may be studying her as avidly as she studies them. The governess watches Flora to learn whether she sees Jessel, and Flora watches the governess for the same reason. The governess arises in the night and thinks she sees someone; Flora does the same. Flora arises and looks out a window; the governess does the same. When Miles asks about going to school, he complains to the governess that she never tells what she thinks. He also wants to know what she has told his uncle (57). These observations, as well as the elaborate prank, indicate that the children see the governess as having a secret about which she is silent. In their way they may be trying to discover what it is.

Whatever the cause of their behavior, the governess seems justified in becoming suspicious and in trying to discover what is behind
it. What she discovers stirs her doubts as much as it does our own.

The governess anticipates her own psychoanalysis by seeing herself from society's perspective. The most common explanation of her
unconscious motives for turning her attention to the children is that
the governess transfers her impossible love for the master to Miles.
Critics point to Miles's being in several ways a young double of his
uncle, wearing clothes like the master's and having something of his
bearing. Much is made of the comparison she uses to describe their
last meal: afterwards they were as silent "as some young couple who,
on their wedding-journey, at the inn, feel shy in the presence of the
waiter" (81). In this reading her banishing Quint to darkness and silence may represent the moment of transferring her desire from the
uncle to the young master. She must exile the image of desire because
the boy is not a possible sexual object. Her desire is not banished,
however; it is only made invisible and silent. Therefore, it comes out
in ghosts saying what she is forbidden to say. What she cannot say to
the master or the children, the ghosts say to the children when she
cannot hear. Their desire to possess the children shows her unconscious desire to possess them, but especially Miles, as substitutes for
the master.

The governess's conscious desires to possess the children and to
preserve their innocence cover her unconscious desire to enter with
them into the sorts of relations she imagines they continue with Quint
and Jessel. As she becomes convinced that all four meet perpetually in
unholy communion, she unconsciously wants to join in. Her increas-
ing frustration at being shut out of their secret lives, just as she has
been shut out by the uncle, leads to aggressive behavior. She grows
unconsciously to hate them and proceeds finally to hurt them.

While this is a plausible reading of her unconscious, it is not the
only persuasive reading. Felman and Brooke-Rose suggest that the
governess's unconscious desires focus more on herself than on the uncle after she expels Quint. She no longer dreams of the master coming
to Bly, but instead concentrates her energies upon discovering what

the children know. There is ample evidence that after she ceases to see the ghosts, she soon becomes more interested in seeing than in being seen.

Perhaps rather than communing with the children and the ghosts, she really wants to see what the children see. From the beginning she has seen herself as an adult who can bear to look upon evil to spare children from looking on it. Her society tells her that adults should know and understand evil, but that children should not. When she ceases to see ghosts, this correct order is reversed. Before Flora's first stand at the window, the governess had alternated between her fantasy visions of a perfect love and her nightmare visions of guilty fornication. Now she is allowed to see only the perfect surface while she believes the children can see beneath it. Whereas before she confusedly moved into the point of view and attitude of Quint, now she searches for access to the children's point of view, for like the ghosts before, the children now seem to stand in her rightful position. Her conscious need is to achieve verification of her reading, to learn whether the children meet the ghosts. Might she unconsciously desire to restore her own visions?

Some of her observations suggest that she envies the children's experience. During their last month, they repeatedly approach forbidden subjects: the children's past and the return of the dead. To her the children seem to know she wants to talk of these things but dares not. She feels they are watching her as intently as she watches them. In manipulating her, pulling "the strings of my invention and my memory," they analyzed her while she failed to penetrate them (51). She says that though she was glad to be spared visions of the ghosts, she suffered in her belief that the children were seeing. On occasions when she was sure the ghosts were among them, though she could not see them, she trembled "with the fear of their addressing to their younger victims some yet more infernal message or more vivid image than they had thought good enough for myself" (53). She goes on, "What it was least possible to get rid of was the cruel idea that whatever I had seen, Miles and Flora saw *more*—things terrible and unguessable and that sprang from dreadful passages of intercourse in the past" (53). In this reading she joins her readers in attempting to decipher the secret message in one part of the chain of repeated communications we saw in the prologue. She wants to know what the dead have to say.

Though her envious tone is almost certainly ironic, it nevertheless suggests that unconsciously the governess may want to see what she believes the children see. What the governess consciously experiences as a need to speak about the forbidden may be a manifestation of her unconscious desire to look upon it. By expelling Quint into silence and darkness, she may have successfully handled her unconscious physical desires, signaling her acceptance of the reality of the uncle's indifference and of her socially determined identity as a virtuous young woman. These desires may emerge in another way, however, as a sort of pornographic impulse. If she gives up the actual object of desire, she can perhaps continue to handle it by symbolic means. If the children witness "dreadful passages of intercourse," then they may see images of the very desires she has given up. For this reason, she may wish to appropriate their point of view, mad as she thinks it is. It becomes useful for her to read the children as possessed by Quint and Jessel. This becomes an unconscious reason for keeping other authorities clear of the scene and for wanting to talk with the children about the ghosts.

This reading also helps account for the return of Jessel after Miles strikes out for freedom. When the governess returns home alone after Miles's announcement, she plans to run away. Meeting Jessel in the schoolroom convinces her to remain, reminding her that the children's souls are at issue. There are suggestions in this apparition of an unconscious motive as well. The incident seems to begin with the governess collapsing on the bottom step in despair, only to remember that she last saw Jessel there. When she actually sees Jessel, she finds the spirit in the governess's position in the schoolroom. As she looks at Jessel in possession, she feels a contest between them over who really belongs: "she had looked at me long enough to appear to say that her right to sit at my table was as good as mine to sit at hers" (59). The governess even speaks to Jessel: "You terrible miserable woman!" (59) She later tells Mrs. Grose that for all practical purposes she and Jessel have conversed. The governess has learned that Jessel suffers the torments of the damned and wants Flora to share them (60–61). This is the governess's grandest and most charitable view of either ghost, including as it does, some pity. Is this pity part of an unconscious recognition of herself in Jessel?

Unconsciously, the governess may recognize Jessel as an image of her forbidden and expelled desire for the master. Furthermore, she may see that leaving the field to Jessel would amount to transforming herself, to becoming Jessel. How would this transformation occur?

Unconsciously, if she cannot act out her passion for the master, then perhaps she can at least appropriate and integrate Jessel, the image of her desire. Having expelled her desire by making the ghosts invisible, she then tries to handle it indirectly, through the children. Miles's bid for freedom threatens to deprive her of unconscious, indirect access to this image. As a result direct access returns. Now the governess and Jessel find themselves in an equal and absolute combat, in the sense that only one of them can be allowed to be real. If the governess leaves, she in effect becomes Jessel, for Jessel is left in her place. Therefore she must remain and struggle.

The governess in this confrontation unconsciously experiences herself as split into two persons; her unconscious desire stands before her as Jessel. This split cannot be allowed to remain, for it will lead to psychosis, a governess with two personalities. If she remains, she confronts her split self without knowing what she is doing. She cannot flee, because her unconscious self is part of her; it will follow in some way. She can hold herself together only by continuing the struggle to dominate Jessel.

The governess's drive to dispossess the children is fueled by an unconscious desire to appropriate to herself what is only available from their point of view, a vision of her wholeness. When the children threaten to escape her control, she once again experiences herself as she did before expelling Quint from the house, as splitting apart. She then struggles to maintain her wholeness by preserving control over the children. The interest of this reading is enhanced when we remember that the children appear to be trying to occupy her perspective.

There is more concrete evidence that the children are studying the governess than that they are communing with ghosts. Perhaps both the governess and the children are attempting to appropriate images of their own wholeness in the eyes of those who love them. The governess, at least, has had an opportunity to discover the reality of her unconscious in her visions; perhaps she goes from there to take control of and integrate it by means of the children.

LORD, YOU DO CHANGE!: ANALYZING THE ANALYSIS

While this reading of the governess has much to recommend it, it has brought us to an apparent contradiction. We have arrived at the conclusion that perhaps the governess's discovery that the children converse with the ghosts results from her unconscious desire to know her unconscious. How can she have an unconscious desire to know her unconscious? To answer this question, we will have to revise our interpretation of the governess's unconscious motives.

We have said that the governess begins to see ghosts when she represses her physical desire for the uncle. Quint represents that desire as outside herself and forbidden. When her desire for the master becomes strong enough, Quint appears. Then Jessel appears as an image of what the governess would be were her secret desire satisfied. She seems to gain control over this situation by gaining control over her desires. She ceases to see ghosts and gives up her fantasy of union with the master. It appears she may accomplish this by transferring her desire to the children. This is the point at which we encounter difficulty. We find that she does not, in fact, begin to treat the children as she has been treating the uncle. They do not take his place as objects of her desire to be seen and approved. Instead, they seem to become mediums for her. She unconsciously wishes to occupy their points of view, to see what she believes they see. Her conscious reason for this is to save them from the ghosts. On this level the ghosts are her rivals for possession of the children. But unconsciously she wants to see the ghosts through their eyes. We have seen this impulse earlier, when it was confusedly present to her that she should place herself where Quint had stood outside the dining room window. Then she wanted to occupy his point of view, to see herself as he saw her.

Noticing this connection suggests that her early vague wish to see herself from the ghost's point of view has blossomed into a more insistent desire to see herself from the children's point of view. At this point we see her apparently governed by an unconscious wish to look upon her unconscious. Now let us reexamine her movement from a slightly different point of view.

Though it is reasonable to think that the governess's repressed physical desires were central motives for first seeing the ghosts, we recall that her fantasies were not about sexual activity. We concluded that they must be about sexual desire because of Mrs. Grose's account of the Quint and Jessel relationship and because popular Freudian analysis has a tendency to place repressed sexual desires at the center of unconscious motivation. The governess actually dreams of being seen and approved. She wants to be visible to the uncle even though he commands that she be silent and invisible. What if we interpret the ghosts as unconscious answers to her conscious desire to be seen?

In her fantasies the governess dwells in the realm of the imaginary. She imagines herself worthy of the loving gaze of the uncle because she has constructed a new, expanded self at Bly and has achieved a harmonious equilibrium within herself and with her new circumstances. We have seen that she is mistaken about her worthiness on these grounds.

The *imaginary* is a technical term in Lacanian psychoanalysis.[18] It refers to what Lacan called the mirror phase in the infant's development of a self. In this phase the child moves from a disorganized self to an idea of itself as whole, then loses that vision of wholeness. During this phase the infant imagines that it and its mother form a single, continuous, all-encompassing whole. This phase comes to an end when the child realizes that mother and child are two beings rather than one. The stage is then set for the Oedipal phase, when the child discovers that it cannot satisfy the mother's needs and, partly in response to this inadequacy, forms a gender identity.

The governess in her fantasies seems to repeat aspects of the mirror phase, though from a more adult self-awareness. She reveals a desire for imaginary unity in which she is perfect and all is under her control. The uncle's seeing her would be the proof of her achievement. The ghosts reveal that she is not in control and that she is not the unity she dreams of being. Nevertheless, they seem to work for her insofar as they locate the main disturbances of her desired unity outside herself. They coincide and conspire with her fantasy, for she can continue to think of herself as a whole being persecuted by external enemies.

The governess's conscious desire to be seen, then, may point to her unconscious desire to repeat the beginning of her mirror phase. Being seen confers imaginary wholeness upon the infant. According to Lacan, the infant by some means sees its own body as a whole and recognizes with intense pleasure the possibility of completeness. Then it transfers this idea to its psychological identity. The mirroring look of the mother confirms the child's wholeness by seeming to see it as it wants to be seen. This look thus becomes a source of continuing joy.

After the illusion of wholeness is lost at the end of the mirror phase, the child begins to seek the look of love, first in the mother's eyes, then in the eyes of the world. If it is not whole, it still hopes to be sufficient, to be the only one the mother needs. The first happiness of discovering one's identity becomes the pattern of seeking happiness in this stage and throughout life. When the child learns it cannot be one, it tries to be the other of two, but then it learns in the Oedipal phase that both mothers and fathers are necessary to create children. Having discovered that it is one of three and not sufficient for its mother, it begins a movement into the adult world, in search of the love of others.

We want to be loved in part in order to repeat the pleasurable experience of first imagining ourselves as psychologically unified beings. In this way the governess is just like all people whom we judge to be normal. In seeking the look of love, she affirms her humanity. That she wishes to earn love by loving shows her to be rather a mature person. Why, then, do things seem to go wrong?

When we look at her desire from this point of view, we are forced to attend more closely to the uncle's prohibition. By insisting upon the condition of her silence, he has made her invisible. He pointedly refuses to look at her, telling her she can earn his love by disappearing. This demand is irresponsible. Though the children have been thrust upon him, still they are his family. If he continues his gay bachelor life, they will be the heirs of his estate, but he wants little to do with them. By commanding her silence, he makes the governess a screen between himself and the children, making them invisible too. He uses her without consideration of her or the children's legitimate needs.

His command that she disappear, reenforced by his handling of the headmaster's letter and by his subsequent absence, may be seen to lead to her hallucinations or, at least, to her reading the ghosts as she does. If she loves him and if she experiences her desire to be seen as a form of repetition of her original experience of becoming visible in the mirror phase, then so absolute a denial of her desire may threaten her with disintegration. Lacan characterizes the premirror phase, roughly the first six months after birth, as the experience of oneself as fragments, parts of the body and of the world in unrelated and uncontrollable presence. When the governess fragments into images and projections—the ghosts, the children, the uncle, and Mrs. Grose—then she is undergoing an experience analogous to her premirror phase. She comes apart under the pressure of the uncle's refusal to look at or hear her.

The ultimate disappearance is death, and this turns out to be the issue when the governess expels Quint from the house. The ghosts insistently raise for her the question of who really belongs. Quint's challenges are pointedly territorial. When she meets Quint on the stairs, the issue seems to be who will be dead. The governess chooses life for her consciousness. She chooses not to disappear and asserts her superiority over what she may only unconsciously recognize as herself in fragments. How can she do this? If she needs the gaze of a beloved to make her whole or, at least, to feel sufficient, how can she assert her wholeness in the absence of this gaze?

It is important to remember that the governess is not an infant;

she is repeating a pattern established in her infancy rather than inventing it. If she cannot achieve the pleasure of wholeness under the uncle's eye, then she may turn to making herself whole. This, of course, is exactly what we have seen her do after expelling the ghosts. Then she no longer wants the uncle to come to Bly, because she has taken it upon herself to be master. Indeed, because he will not look, his mastery has become inadequate. He will not see what she has seen and, therefore, would be a threat to her mastery were he to come.

In this reading of the governess's unconscious, her asserting power over the ghosts becomes a crucial turning point in her adventure. When she shifts attention from the ghosts to the children, she also moves from passivity to activity. She has passively awaited the master's look of approval until his refusal threatened her with annihilation. Now she actively seeks the master's privileged point of view; she will try to see through his eyes. Her conscious intention becomes to possess the children, to keep them out of the ghosts' clutches. Behind her conscious purpose is an unconscious intention to appropriate the children's point of view. Her unconscious goal is not precisely, as we said before, to see her unconscious, but rather to see herself whole. Knowing secrets is not an end in itself as we suggested when we speculated that she had a kind of pornographic urge to participate vicariously in the intercourse of Quint and Jessel. Rather, the governess's desire to see herself whole seems to entail occupying a point of view outside herself.

This need to see with the eyes of the children in order to see with the eyes of the master seems puzzling, but we must remember that this master is not the real uncle. The master is an imaginary character upon whom the governess has conferred the power of seeing her whole. Any point of view from which she can catch a glimpse of herself as unified is the master's position. The governess, unable consciously to find the gaze of love, unconsciously tries to construct it. She unconsciously and desperately tries to love herself.

What the governess unconsciously wants is impossible. Her wholeness is imaginary. No one can achieve perfect unity, because the unconscious always remains a quasi-alien part of the self. She has conceived this impossible desire as a natural response to falling in love with a man who refuses to acknowledge her, and this desire is a deadly trap not of her own making.

She is trapped because the uncle has inadvertently made her believe in the possibility of mastery. He has blinded her to the fact that his point of view really is inadequate. By commanding her to take charge fully, he implies that obedience is possible. Even though she knows consciously that he would misread Bly were he present, she still maintains an unconscious faith in the possibility of reading Bly correctly. She continues to believe in the privileged position of a mythical master. She acts as if there is a point of view from which the whole truth can be known, just as rereaders act when they begin to see the multiple perspectives in the prologue. Consciously believing the children communicate with the ghosts, she unconsciously concludes that they have access to the master point of view she desires.

She comes to believe consciously that she can master the situation at Bly by appropriating the children's point of view. If she sees what they see, she will see it all. Then she will save the children from the ghosts, possess herself completely, and—if the opportunity arises—present herself to the uncle as sufficient, worthy of his love whether or not he deigns to give it.

On the unconscious level, possessing herself completely is a deeper and knottier problem than she can know. She appears on this level to be trying to articulate the ineffable meaning of symbolic figures; the children become letters of the text of her unconscious. If she can read them, she can gain conscious possession of her wholeness and master herself. Her unconscious aims are dangerously harmonious with her conscious aims.

This harmony increases her danger, for it keeps her blind to the workings of unconscious motives in her choices, as revealed in her final actions. At this point we can see how her unconscious motives press her attention to the children. She comes to believe that they know what she wants to know. On the conscious level they know the forbidden evil that can destroy them. On the unconscious level, they see what is invisible of her self. She believes if she can just pass the barriers of their silence and of the prohibitions of her society, she will be able to save them. Focusing on these visible barriers keeps her unaware that passing them will not give her what she unconsciously wants. Like the barriers and perspectives in the prologue, these obstructions and promises of aid sustain her in the illusion that her new version of imaginary wholeness is really attainable. But, each symbolic figure she encounters actually hides the meaning it seems to reveal. The mastery of meaning is always deferred to another figure. She looks from one to another in endless succession without discovering the promised view that attracts her gaze.

In her first experience of adult love, the governess finds herself pushed back into childhood, and she may be seen as repeating the strategies that worked then. Conceiving herself as whole, she longs for the beloved's confirming gaze. The failure of the gaze threatens to disintegrate her, so she begins to make the effort to be sufficient. This effort leads to her trying to possess herself by establishing control over her invisible self. In her present situation, such an effort is a trap. The unconscious patterns by which she tries to grow into a fully adequate self are too congruent with actual events at Bly. That the children have a secret plays into her unconscious quest. Her desire energizes her conscious quest to save the children, tempting her to rashness and probably distorting what she concludes about the content of their secret. As a result, the children are endangered.

Thus we see the normal flow of her growth, dammed near its source by the uncle, overflowing into the streams of the children, where it is again dammed by social convention and their silence. Perforce she must imagine the invisible channels her energy would follow were it released. Or, put another way, the secret of her being is in a box in a room with windows and a door. This secret is unknowable and the box is imaginary, but she cannot know this because the door (the master) and the windows (the children) are closed. Looking at them she never even glimpses the empty space where she believes the box to rest.

We have turned radically away from the traditional psychoanalytic interpretation of the governess. The hypothesis that she is sexually frustrated seems inadequate to account for her banishing the ghosts and shifting attention to the children in the way she does. This does not mean, of course, that sexual frustration has nothing to do with the apparitions. Until this key event, sexual desire seemed quite an adequate way of explaining why she might need to imagine ghosts. Now, however, we have moved to a perspective in which sexual desire may not be seriously present at all or may be at most a relatively minor aspect of a more fundamental desire to achieve wholeness by being loved.

The procedure I have followed may seem rather strange. Why did I not begin a psychoanalytic interpretation of the governess with this idea instead of deceiving the reader about my aims and detouring through the traditional reading? Thoughtful readers will see several reasons for my perfidy, but I want to emphasize just one here.

Psychoanalysis, from my layman's point of view, is much more an art than a science. Because it uses models, close observation, and a form of experimentation, it often seems more certain of its conclusions than is warranted by actual cases. I believe that I had a quite persuasive case going for sexual frustration as the key to reading the governess's unconscious. Therefore, I take a certain measure of delight in pulling out of the magic hat quite a different key here. Furthermore, I anticipate more delight as other readers—more sophisticated, more informed, or more foolish—revise and correct my reading, until perhaps keys will start like rabbits. My delight arises, of course, from the apparent helplessness of psychoanalysis to yield certainty about the governess's unspoken motives. Even with this fascinating tool we cannot enter the box of her unconscious.

9

The Last Act of My Dreadful Drama

We have arrived at our last opportunity to achieve certainty about Miles and Flora's fate. In this chapter, still looking for the key to this tale, we examine their final meetings with the governess.

Though we have energetically invented persuasive speculation about the governess's unconscious motives, we have not been able to prove that the governess hallucinates or misinterprets what she sees. Our analysis of her secrets is unable to achieve significantly greater authority than her own analysis of the children. We can show that she may be wrong, and we can show that our psychoanalysis may be wrong. Certainty eludes us.

In this chapter we look at the governess's actions to save the children. Fully aware of her own uncertainty, the governess delays acting as long as she believes she can. When she acts, the children are visibly damaged. Perhaps by examining her actions carefully, we can determine who is responsible for harming the children. Once again, we aim for that elusive certainty.

A FIGURE PORTENTOUS: FLORA AND JESSEL

In the governess's final meeting with Flora and Jessel, James turns his screw with appalling power, as might be shown in a minor but telling way by the number of times the word *turn* appears in chapters 20 and 21. We encounter vivid visions that force a rapid alternation between the two main perspectives. A list will help to illustrate this pattern.

Flora at the Lake and After

1. While Miles diverts the governess, Flora escapes out of doors, rows across the lake, and hides the boat.
2. When the governess and Mrs. Grose find her, the governess asks where Jessel is.
3. Jessel appears, and the governess is justified.
4. Mrs. Grose does not see, Flora denies seeing, and the governess's position crumbles.
5. Mrs. Grose takes charge of Flora overnight.
6. The next morning Mrs. Grose reports a transformation in Flora that she thinks could only be the result of her communing with evil.
7. Mrs. Grose, promising to support the governess against Flora's charges, takes Flora to her uncle.

The children conspiring, and the strangeness, elaborateness, and physical difficulty—an eight-year-old rowing and secluding a boat—of this escape reaffirm the children's unnatural precociousness. Jessel's appearance in Mrs. Grose's presence seems to settle the matter; with relief we drop into acceptance of the governess's point of view. To know she is right is as much a relief for us as for her. We have wanted to know the truth. She wished not merely to be sane and justified, but above all to love the children.

When Mrs. Grose fails to see and Flora denies that she sees, our position crumbles too, and we find ourselves looking at the governess with the eyes of the skeptical master. Which is the real governess? Is she who she says she is, or has she unknowingly become Jessel, opening an innocent child's imagination to representations of evil? Flora's response to the governess's invocation of Jessel is to place the governess in Jessel's place, to demand that the governess never again come near her.

Having absorbed this revolution from uncertainty to certainty to deeper doubt, we are brought up again with the governess when Mrs. Grose confirms the transformation the governess saw in Flora. Mrs. Grose reports that Flora has become old, that she takes a high manner, placing herself socially and morally above the governess, and that she uses language that could only have come from evil people. These observations lead Mrs. Grose to affirm that though she has seen no other evidence she believes the governess's version of events and will support it before the master.

When Mrs. Grose once again stands "shoulder to shoulder" with the governess, we are left where we began, in doubt about which interpretation has greater weight (78). Like the organization of this confrontation, the details also contribute to an effect of intellectual and emotional whiplash.

The governess reads into Flora's excursion the same meaning she saw in Miles's request to return to school. Flora, too, is tacitly acknowledging that she and the governess are aware of a secret that puts the governess at a disadvantage. Therefore, Flora can demand more freedom and privacy. The governess decides she cannot allow this because it means turning Flora over to Jessel. For this reason she speaks what she believes is the secret, asking where Jessel is. As if called, Jessel appears vividly to the governess. Here is one of the crucial points at which the governess fails to read Mrs. Grose, for she believes Mrs. Grose also sees. Believing Mrs. Grose is looking at Jessel, the governess looks at Flora, who becomes a "figure portentous," as she turns "at *me* an expression of hard still gravity, an expression absolutely new and unprecedented and that appeared to read and accuse and judge me" (71). Flora offers herself to be read in a new way, but how?

The governess reads Flora's reaction as studied denial. Flora expresses exactly the attitude that any reasonable adult would adopt in response to the governess's assertion that the children are communing with evil spirits. This is the attitude that has held the governess in check until this crisis. The governess insists that Flora can at that moment see Jessel and is convinced that Flora has adopted an attitude that is revealed in her not glancing toward Jessel's continuing display. The governess's insistence leads Flora to complete the adoption of her manner. Then Mrs. Grose announces that she sees nothing and comforts Flora with the assurance that, of course, she too sees nothing. Only then does Flora respond to the accusation: "I don't know what you mean. I see nobody. I see nothing. I never *have*. I think you 're cruel. I don't like you!" (73).

We see a double transformation. Flora's behavior suggests that the governess, by mentioning Jessel, becomes for Flora the evil governess. Likewise Flora, in denying intercourse with Jessel, becomes Jessel in the governess's eyes. From the other's point of view, each becomes domineering, old, common, ugly, hard, and cruel. Though the affection between them before this ought to provide a deep reserve for continued conversation, this topic absolutely separates them.

If Flora's reaction is pretense, it is quite sophisticated, possible only on the assumption of the influence of "some outside force" (73). But even if it is not studied, it seems much more adult than one would expect of an eight-year-old. What does her reaction mean?

The governess's reading is clear enough. When forced to choose between them, Flora has chosen the evil mother figure. If evil has become Flora's good, then to her the good governess is evil. Flora's transformation reflects the influence of Jessel. The governess's reading is supported by changes in Flora's behavior. Even to Mrs. Grose Flora is markedly a different person by the next morning. The governess, therefore, sees herself as right in her reading, but mistaken in her tactics. She waited too long to act: "I' ve done my best, but I' ve lost you" (73). We may notice the imagery of warfare and catastrophe in their encounter and wonder if the governess is too violent.

The reasons for doubting the governess's reading are also quite clear. Equivocal though it is, Flora's denial when combined with Mrs. Grose's throws us back upon the governess's subjectivity. Only she sees, and her reading is privileged because she is in power. We may consider Flora's point of view. Since her response rather precisely mirrors the governess's, we see more evidence that Flora's perspective resembles the governess's. One speculative version of Flora's experience is that she has discovered in the governess's odd behavior a silence and has filled it with her own desires. Out of that silence comes what for Flora is a horrifying surprise, the accusation of communing with Jessel, a reopening of the old terror.

What might Flora have wished to find in the governess's secret place? Given Flora's history of losing parental figures, she might want a more stable and complete family. In the previous weeks, when the unspoken seemed to the governess to be in the air, the children always brought up the hoped for visit from the uncle and usually wrote him a letter. Mrs. Grose's accounts hint that for Flora, Jessel is not a pleasant memory. That the children never speak of Quint and Jessel may point to their own repression of a painful relationship or at least of the loss of more parents. Their unnatural goodness may derive from their desire to attach the governess to them as part of recreating their family. We might even speculate about how their development has been disturbed from a Lacanian point of view. How often have they lost the gaze of love and proven insufficient to their caretakers. How do they respond to their uncle's averted gaze?

Perhaps the escapades were intended to provoke the governess to act on what they believed was her secret wish to marry the uncle. When Flora takes her step, she receives a surprise, not the image of married parents and a mother restored, but the accusation of intercourse with the repressed evil mother. Flora's transformation would result from the breakdown of her delicate repression of Jessel's image. She "becomes" Jessel not because she has been communing with ghosts, but because the governess names her predecessor. Her transformation may reveal the "other mother" Flora has repeatedly experienced, the cruel one who loves another and then abandons her. That Flora's behavior suggests some deep mental disturbance is shown by its being split. On the one hand, she takes on the manner of a lady quite superior to the governess, yet on the other hand, she uses common and vulgar language.

Though there is some evidence on which to build these hypotheses, they are almost completely speculative. The main point is that there are plausible ways to construe Flora's behavior in her final scenes that have virtually nothing to do with what the governess believes. Because we have more knowledge of the governess's history, we can construct more convincing readings of her reading. Why might she imagine Jessel's last appearance in the way she does?

Flora's escape from the house with Miles's help repeats Miles's earlier escape with Flora's aid. The cycle that has separated the governess from Miles seems now to be under way for Flora. Therefore, the governess's chances of appropriating the children's visions are slipping away. For this reason, she strikes quickly and violently. If she is to use the children to appropriate and dominate her unconscious, then she must make them have visions before they escape her. The congruence of her unconscious and conscious desires produces a rash response to a moment of crisis. So she forces upon Flora the vision of Jessel. Failing to impose her perspective upon either Flora or Mrs. Grose, she collapses.

The governess's urge to complete her identity has been defeated by Flora's refusal to yield up the image of the governess's unconscious. It may be ironic that this scene surrounds the governess with images of her unconscious. She, Jessel, and Flora all mirror each other. The governess is unable to recognize that this collection of images is what she seeks. To the governess Jessel seems wholly other. She cannot domesticate this figure. She cannot allow it to represent something within herself but apart from her conscious identity. Even were she to recognize the figure, she would grasp not meaning, but rather another symbol. She once turned her look from Jessel to Flora only to have it turned back again. She cannot appropriate herself by imposing a perspective on Flora, just as Flora may not have been able to appropriate herself by means of the governess.

Nor can we readers "see it all" by imposing our readings upon the governess. The governess's final attempt with Flora seems to show three of the major actors in this dreadful drama reflecting each other's dilemma. None can attain a final view by means of another. The whole of any person and, therefore, of the situation repeatedly defines itself as more than meets the eye. The governess sees her tale as a drama, with a whole beginning and a last act, but her attempts to make it whole have not satisfied her, nor do they satisfy us.

BLIND WITH VICTORY: MILES AND QUINT

When Miles volunteers the names of Jessel and Quint, apparently un-prompted by anyone, he provides the strongest evidence the governess can offer that he has spoken with their spirits. It parallels Mrs. Grose's speaking the names, which is the strongest proof that the governess sees real ghosts. Miles's behavior here suggests that he really expects to see one or both of the ghosts and that he really believes the govern-ess sees Quint. That he seems to call Quint a devil confirms the gov-erness's opinion that the ghosts are evil. That he believes in Quint's presence without seeing him tends to verify that Miles's decision to confess is tantamount to rejecting the demonic influence in favor of the governess's. These events, supported by all that has come before, are the governess's justification for asserting that she has saved Miles, even though he died of being saved.

Once again we meet with a chance at certainty. Here is a report unequivocally establishing that Miles is aware of the presence of Jes-sel, the one he names without significant prompting. But as we take in this evidence, we also encounter the governess's doubts, expressed in her taking note of her rashness. And we hardly have time to savor the comfort of being sure before we reencounter or remember Miles's death and the governess's assertion that she has saved him. Our cer-tainty seems to hang on Miles's surrender of the names, for all other evidence is easily challengeable. Most of it the governess has chal-lenged herself. Are Miles's final words enough to establish our faith in the governess's interpretation of events at Bly?

So we have returned to the incident that initiated our rereading. We arrive with a deeper knowledge of the governess's importance. Re-reading has increased our awareness that the governess is not merely a reporter, but also the crucial interpreter of and actor in this drama.

As a narrator at some distance from her actions, the governess has emerged as a reinterpreter, who has anticipated our vacillations. Still, her moral and intellectual sophistication, though they become more visible upon second reading, do not relieve our anxiety. We return to the scene of Miles's death no more sure whether the governess has read Bly correctly.

Of course, if Miles's speaking the names is unequivocal proof of the governess's reading, then our problem is solved. Our vibration between the two main readings can end if his behavior proves the governess right. His speaking is strong proof; psychoanalytic readings have been hard pressed to explain how he speaks those names and why he dies. That Miles heard the names from Flora is quite unlikely, even though they breakfasted together that morning. Mrs. Grose would not have concealed such a conversation from the governess. Shlomith Rimmon points out, however, the ambiguity of Mrs. Grose's statement that she successfully kept the children apart after the lake incident.[19] If Rimmon is right, it becomes possible that the children communicated, but then Miles seems extraordinarily disingenuous in his subsequent conversations with the governess.

If Miles comes to expect apparitions of Quint and Jessel in the governess's presence, though he has never seen them himself, he is much more likely to have conceived this idea based on the governess's behavior and words. If he has never talked of his time with Quint and Jessel, neither has she. She has complained to him of his silence, and he has let her know he feels ignorant of what she thinks about him. He has gone so far as to steal a letter to learn what is on her mind. It would take inspired guessing for him to move from what she has said and not said and from her strange behavior in recent weeks to the conclusion that she sees apparitions of Jessel and perhaps of Quint. But, Miles, next to the governess, is assuredly the most inspired guesser at Bly. As Pemberton says of the older child, Morgan, in James's "The Pupil" (1891), "There was nothing that at a given moment you could say a clever child didn't know." [20]

This leads to another of many ways of constructing the children's point of view. In Flora's last scene, we saw her as possibly attempting to read into the governess's silence a hidden desire for the master that would lead to the reformation of a family. What if the children felt that the governess was making them see Jessel? Whether they saw Quint remains more equivocal; Miles need only associate the two people to think of him when the governess tells him the apparition is not Jessel.

If in their present governess the children saw Jessel, reading her as the possibility of the return of the evil governess, their various activities become explainable as ways of exorcising Jessel, of helping the governess deal with her unconscious. They would do this in part because they prefer the present jolly governess to Jessel.

Then their activities toward her mirror hers toward them: to protect her from seeing, to see in her place, to keep her separated from her unconscious. Flora wants to escape from the governess when the latter seems to become Jessel. Miles becomes angry in the end because he believes he has failed to expel Jessel; the governess possesses or is possessed by her, and he is helpless. His fear of the consequences, added to the other stresses of the situation, prove too much for his sensitive frame.

In this scenario the governess and the children play tragically to each other's losing hands, each with good intentions defeating the other's attempts at self-integration, all trying to deal with their repressions of Jessel. Neither can really understand what the other is doing, for each sees only himself or herself in the other.

This tragic mirroring emphasizes the degree to which what the governess attempts is erroneous when taken out of her implicitly religious perspective. If she is dealing with psychological development rather than with spiritual forces, then the rules of the game are quite different. One controls but does not banish the unconscious, and using images is essential to learning this control. While each may see Jessel as belonging to the other person, each is also reading into Jessel meanings from his or her own unconscious. If the governess deprives the children of the images by which they deal with their unconscious desires, she prevents them from becoming whole, just as it appears her society has prevented her.

This version of the children's point of view would account for their being aware of Jessel's proximity while leaving them innocent of the evil the governess attributes to them. That we can construct at least two plausible readings of the children that the governess never thought of undercuts the governess's reading. The children's silence makes them appear as symbols into which many meanings can be read. By reading them as she does, the governess tends to exclude their point of view.

The possibility that Miles has read the governess as successfully as she has read him and our speculations about the children's point of view tend to undercut the persuasiveness of her testimony about Miles's last words. Nevertheless, her account stubbornly contradicts our many doubts about her interpretations. Still, we never escape her being the only witness to Miles's confession and the ghostly manifestations. No matter how much we have come to trust the governess's perceptions and to give ample weight to her interpretations, we are prevented from giving them absolute authority. Though Miles's speaking the names is less equivocal than any other evidence in the governess's favor, except perhaps her giving Mrs. Grose physical descriptions of the ghosts, still that evidence comes at the end of an accumulation of doubt that cannot be silenced, is accompanied by the governess's own doubts about some aspects of her action, and is followed by the enormous doubt we feel concerning Miles's fate. Even the most minor possibilities of alternate explanations contribute to this doubt about Miles's words.

The governess's doubts tend to focus not on whether she was right in her reading, but on her method of handling Miles. Once Mrs. Grose, under the influence of Flora's transformation, affirms her faith in her superior, the governess proceeds with little doubt of her own rightness: "I seemed to myself for the instant to have mastered it, to see it all. . . . 'He 'll confess. If he confesses, he 's saved'" (78–79). Her attention turns to the problem of bringing Miles to confess. The immediate occasion of confession is Miles's theft of the letter, a request for an interview she has written to the uncle for the purpose of beginning discussion of finding Miles a school. It is important to notice that the governess does not report herself as selfishly concerned about retaining her position, for some have argued that she is more interested in saving herself and her reputation than in saving Miles. In fact, if she saves Miles, she saves herself, but she must save Miles first. Even if her amply demonstrated love for the children were insincere, she would have to behave as if she loved them to keep from being declared insane or at least perverse.

She hopes that by beginning with the letter, she can move to his expulsion from school and eventually to the ghosts, getting him to lay out completely his unspoken side. As they begin this last conversation, the governess becomes convinced that Miles can no longer see the ghosts and that should either appear she will be able to see it (82). Her main evidence for this change is Miles's restlessness, his eagerness to leave her. She believes that he has not seen Quint since his silent indication on the previous evening of a desire to tell her he has taken the letter. Presumably his decision, in his new freedom, to choose himself rather than be chosen by Quint, has cut him off from communicating with Quint. Seeing this, the governess assures Miles of her affection and that she remains with him now mainly to learn what is on his mind. She believes that each knows what is ahead as he agrees to talk with her.

In the confession that follows, Quint appears twice outside the dining room window, when she asks her first question, whether Miles took the letter, and again when she asks him to specify what "things" he said at school. Her response to the first appearance is to successfully hide it from Miles. When he confesses that he took the letter and found nothing in it, Quint disappears, and the governess feels elated: "the air was clear again and—by my personal triumph—the influence quenched. . . . I felt that the cause was mine and that I should surely get *all*" (86). Confidently she turns to the matter of the school, eliciting that he was "turned out" because he said "things" to those he liked. When she asks him what things he said, Quint appears again, threatening her victory, "as if to blight his confession" (88). The governess never learns what things were said, for Miles seems to guess she is responding to something he cannot see. She lets him see that he cannot see, proving to him that he is free of Quint's influence. He does not respond, however, as she would expect. He surprises her by becoming furious and by giving not Quint's name first, but Jessel's. She describes him as in "a white rage" when he is unable to see anything and when he speaks Quint's name (88). She comforts him when he cannot see: "What does he matter now, my own?—what will he *ever* matter? *I* have you, . . . but he has lost you for ever!" (88). Her claim to possessing Miles is immediately negated when Miles utters the "cry of a creature hurled over an abyss" and dies in her arms.

This scene is quite complex even in the parts I have selected here to summarize, and there are patterns we will look at below that increase this complexity. The governess's interpretation of this event is that she struggles with a demon over a human soul and is victorious; unfortunately, the soul's earthly life is sacrificed in the battle. As sad as this is, it could have been worse.

Though she reports in detail, she does not judge this scene as fully and as explicitly as other confrontations. She records, but does not explore the implications of unexpected developments. She is surprised by Miles's confession that his crime was saying things to people he liked. There are more surprises. He becomes more remote when she expects their intimacy to increase. He expects Jessel rather than Quint to appear. He becomes angry, and he dies. Though she does not record surprise at all these events, we can see that she should have been surprised. These unexpected events undercut her interpretation, yet she leaves them virtually uninterpreted, seizing upon the surrender of the names as her proof. She may be blinded in part by the severe doubt she feels as a result of Miles confessing that he said his things to those he liked. This information leads her for the last time in her narrative to contemplate an inversion of her reading in which Miles is innocent and she is a monster. Then, she seems not to have mastered the situation at all: "It was for an instant confounding and bottomless" (87). Perhaps as much out of this doubt as out of her question about what specific things Miles said comes Quint's reappearance.

The governess records with little explicit interpretation other puzzling details about their confrontation. For example, she reports his physical and mental deterioration during their conversation. She may implicitly interpret this as proof of her own rashness, which she judges explicitly.

From the moment they are alone together, Miles is physically and mentally disturbed. She notices his anxiety. Each embrace reveals new symptoms: fast beating heart, sweating forehead, pale face, apparent lapses of memory, a little "sick headshake," looking confined, breathing hard, and finally the fury, the white rage. Over against these symptoms, she reports and judges her rashness, her desire to master the situation and gain an absolute victory. She says that after Miles had confessed to saying things at school, she ought to have been satisfied for the time: "I ought to have left it there. But I was infatuated—I was blind with victory, though even then the very effect that was to have brought him so much nearer was already that of added separation" (87). When he confesses he said these things to those he liked, she drops again into serious doubt, the possibility that he was innocent. Exploring this doubt, she questions him further. When her asking about the content of the "things" leads to Quint's reappearance, she again vigorously enters the battle, letting her "impulse flame up" to show Miles that she sees and he does not, and forcing him to yield the names: "I was so determined to have all my proof that I flashed into ice to challenge him" (88).

The governess describes Miles's physical and mental suffering and judges her rashness. By implying a connection, she reveals her persistent, unstated fear that she gained her mastery at the cost of Miles's life. She cannot know whether this is true. It may be dispossession alone that killed him. Or it may be, as psychoanalytic readings often assert, that she simply frightened him to death with her claim under already stressful circumstances that ghosts were present. Her uncertainty means that in asserting her mastery, she lost her it.

Even though Miles's naming the ghosts gives the strongest kind of support to the governess's reading, this support is hedged about with doubts, some belonging to the governess, some generated by her, some discovered by us upon rereading. As in every significant scene in the novella, here there is more than meets the eye. There are gaps, silences, and missing connections and multiple ways of filling these blanks to complete the story. These silences draw us toward the governess's unconscious. If she misreads the ghosts, why would she interpret this scene as she does?

In the confrontation with Flora, the governess was desperate and precipitate. She seized her opportunity without a plan, without a sense of what she should do to separate Flora from Jessel. Her unconscious desperation concerned the loss of the children as mirrors. She unconsciously wanted to make them see her whole, so that through them she could possess all of herself. This enterprise must be doomed, for the unconscious is invisible except as it appears before us in portentous figures that we see as uncanny, simultaneously familiar and strange. The self is organized by accommodation rather than by dictatorship.

When the governess confronts Miles, she is much more under control. She has a plan to carry out. But, from the psychoanalytic point of view this control is illusory. Unconsciously, her desire is the same as with Flora, to specify and then appropriate Miles's vision. Having specified it long before this meeting, she appropriates it before they begin to talk, "discovering" that Miles cannot see and that she can. She then tries to keep possession of the vision, to see for herself and prevent his seeing, while leading him to put into words what he has seen. By this means he will give her the vision she unconsciously wants, the complete view of herself.

The impossibility of this attempt is suggested by Miles's becoming more remote from her as she approaches closer to the full vision. Not only does he recede, but he also becomes more and more a mirror of Quint, with his white face, his repeatedly turning toward her and away, his anger, and his final death. While she attempts to grasp both metaphorically and literally his portentous figure, Miles becomes progressively less graspable, moving into the distance occupied by Quint in appearance, behavior, and physical condition. When she finally holds him, she holds a dead body, the figure without its portent. When he seems more to mirror Quint, he seems less to mirror her. As was the case with Flora, however, his mirroring Quint means he mirrors the governess's unconscious, that she is seeing a representation of what she desires. Her problem seems to remain that she cannot recognize this representation as part of herself. She cannot see that Quint, like Miles, figures forth some aspect of her unconscious. While from his own point of view, Miles's surprising answers and behavior may be a combination of simple truth and psychological stress, from the governess's point of view, they play into a pattern by which she is deprived of a last mirror she unconsciously wishes to control.

THE BEAUTY OF HIS AUTHOR'S HAND: WHAT THE GOVERNESS WANTS

Losing Miles as a mirror seems to mean losing forever the opportunity to impose the mirror role upon others. Douglas's summary of her subsequent career suggests that the governess never again saw visions. Does this mean that her experiences with Miles and Flora somehow "cured" her? In her description of the last scene is also a pattern of imprisonment and suffocation. She several times notes that Miles seems to feel imprisoned, apparently as a result of his no longer seeing Quint. Several of his physical symptoms suggest that he feels closed in and deprived of air. This image corresponds to the imagined condition of the unconscious, its energies and desires closed off in some directions and redirected in others, lacking a voice, having to appeal to consciousness by attaching itself to images as a shadowy silence and to appear in the guise of the dead. Has she, then, cut herself off from her unconscious, failing forever to recognize its silence as her own? We return for answers to the prologue, which for a second time becomes an epilogue as well, and we think now about her whole narrative.

We noticed upon first rereading the prologue that there was a chain of mirroring communications that began, we surmised, with the dead speaking to the children. These communications mirrored each other in that each had a concrete manifestation that someone observed and a secret content that no one was able to articulate. We opined that the secret content kept the message on the move, in search of an authoritative reader who could correctly speak for the silence at which each communication pointed. *The Turn of the Screw* presents the last two documents in the chain, and it invites us to attempt being authoritative readers. The governess's narrative, one document in the chain, now proves to be centrally about her attempt to be an authoritative reader. Our question about her has become: Did she read the situation at Bly as it was, or did she make that situation into a mirror in which she unconsciously saw mainly herself?

We have seen that after the events at Bly, the characters continue to seek mirrors in each other, and mirrors continue to fail. The patterns of the whole novella suggest, however, that while this failure is significant, sometimes even tragic, it is not the worst that can happen. It is quite normal for intimate friends to mirror each other comfortably and successfully. Failures are frequent and disturbing, but they rarely end affectionate relationships, except at the final failure of death. In fact, we have seen just two relationships destroyed, and those only possibly because the governess fails to mirror the children faithfully. If failure to mirror successfully leads to the loss of affection, as between the governess and Flora, or to premature death, as between the governess and Miles, then it becomes tragic.

It is no surprise then to see that the governess, in writing her narrative, is still seeking a mirror. She finds that mirror in Douglas. This is apparent both in the circumstances of the narrative's transmission and within the narrative itself, where she frequently calls upon his specific judgments and reminds herself of her responsibilities to him. It seems clear that the governess's ten-year silence was a period of searching and discovery. She wanted not merely to find the right reader, for she explored her story for herself, trying to discover in it what continued to elude her. What she discovered was plainly that she must tell someone, not just anyone, but someone whom she liked and who liked her. Furthermore, she found that she must tell the whole story, the parts she understood as well as the parts she did not, her judgments at the time and her judgments since. How else can she make clear her problem, that there are blanks, silences, and mysteries in her story that she cannot fathom? She needs an authoritative reader, who can see and articulate a true picture of her self.

According to our psychoanalysis, her need for this reader cannot remain so desperate as it appeared at Bly, for she is patient, meticulous, and careful not to impose, choosing a reader more her equal than the children were. She seems to want to understand whether she was responsible for Miles's death and, therefore, whether she read Bly correctly. She has had to act to save children she believed in danger, and the consequences have been painfully equivocal. Her telling the story at all shows she remains in doubt, especially when we notice how she willingly opens herself to judgment. Her telling it to someone she likes indicates that she wants not a perfectly objective judgment, but a loving one.

A loving judgment is not reductive. If Douglas loves her, he will not simply deny her unspoken side but will give her another perspective on it. Likewise, he will not reduce her to her unconscious motivation as psychoanalytic readings tend to do, portraying her as a mere victim of sexual and identity problems. Instead, he will acknowledge her conscious point of view. Douglas's actual response, insofar as we know it, consists of continuing to love her through his silence and in his telling. This response suggests that he cannot speak for her silence except by repeating her narrative. He mirrors her only by repeating her actions. The screw turns once more.

By speaking for their silence, the governess may have failed to love the children, yet she has loved them in the best way she could find. Believing them in danger, she has struggled for their souls. If she is a blind child leading blind children, this is because her society and education have taught her to remain ever a child herself, then placed upon her the responsibility of preserving the childhood of others. Not knowing herself, she is expected to keep children from discovering themselves. No one is to traffic with the dead, no one to see the silences that hover over the omissions and repressions of Victorian culture. Her narrative is proof that she herself is not satisfied. She continues to believe that there might have been a better way to act.

Her writing to Douglas when she does in the way she does hints that she also suspects her reading of Bly. Douglas, however, cannot confirm it. Silence manifests itself in unreadable symbols.

There is no "cure" for the governess. The conscious/unconscious split of the human psyche can never be healed without ending personal identity in madness or death. But, the governess may achieve an integration of her self, a recognition and acceptance of the unconscious as a part of her whole self. Of course, if she was right all along in her reading of Bly, then her very ability to doubt herself shows the recognition and acceptance of her own unfathomable mystery. If she read her unconscious into Bly, then she may have taken it back to herself by writing it down. If she confesses, perhaps she is saved. Her paper was blank, and would have taken the impression of any tale she might have chosen to tell. She chose to tell her story without touching up, with the facts and impressions that told both for and against her reading. She acknowledged that she knew then and continued to remember that quite opposite readings were possible. She presented the facts she could not explain. In short, she put all she thought important of her adventure on the page. The result was as it should be if she is honest. There is more than meets the eye in her pages. Shadows and silences loom behind her images and words.

In her narrative the governess has constructed a true mirror of herself. It shows her fully to us, pointing to her invisible features as well as showing her visible character. In her narrative she is whole, though still divided. Though her unconscious remains silent and invisible to her and to us, she has appropriated it in a legitimate if ultimately unsatisfactory way by writing her story. If she cannot interpret her images, she can at least represent them on the mirror of the manuscript page.

"I must have thrown myself, on my face, to the ground" (73).
Illustration by Eric Pape, from *Collier's Weekly* 20, no. 26 (2 April 1898):17.
Courtesy of the New York State Historical Association Library.

10

Reading the Unreadable: Meaning in *The Turn of the Screw*

To Catch Those Not Easily Caught

In his preface to the New York Edition, James characterized *The Turn of the Screw* as a piece of "cold artistic calculation, an *amusette* to catch those not easily caught, . . . the jaded, the disillusioned, the fastidious" (NCE 120). It appears as a toy, a minor amusement like telling ghost stories before the fire at Christmas, but at its end *The Turn of the Screw* returns upon itself, refusing to end in the customary way. The tale insists upon its own unresolved ambiguity. We do not know what Miles's death means. Upon rereading, we discover depths of beauty and uncertainty in the governess that leave our attitude toward her changed, but provide no escape from ambiguity. The jaded think this just another easy thriller. The disillusioned, perhaps, find ghost stories boring. The fastidious expect to be able to spot weaknesses that will reveal the story's utter fictionality. James, however, breaks out somewhere else, by forcing our attention away from reading the ghosts and the children with the governess to reading the governess herself. Having made this move, he has caught his readers. We are caught in the ambiguous, double view of the governess and the children.

This view is like the optical illusion of a drawing that could be either two heads profiled and facing each other or a vase. Try as we might from our normal visual perspectives and assumptions, we cannot see both the faces and the vase at once. Likewise, we cannot accept both readings simultaneously, because they are mutually exclusive. There is no compromise reading in which the governess is both right and wrong about whether she saved Miles.

In *The Delights of Terror* I call this feature of the tale *anticlosure,* the refusal of the work to produce or directly suggest its own ending.[21] We saw upon completing the rereading that we were not finished, that even after a second examination, the last events lead us again to the prologue, which contains an implicit epilogue, but which still insists upon becoming a prologue again.

In American and European literature different kinds of fiction have tended to produce their own particular kinds of closure. In general, those not structured as apologues or fables present us with characters about whom we are made to care and with alternative fates for those characters, some of which we come to prefer. The work ends when the characters come to or fail to achieve the preferred fate—"the prince carried her off to his land." The ending may be signaled as well by a tying up of loose ends that projects the fates or life experiences of various characters—"and they lived happily ever after." Perhaps the most familiar form is the quest for a valuable object, marriage, or—what the governess wants—knowledge. From the moment she first sees Quint, she pursues sufficient knowledge to be certain how she should act, but she never learns enough. For the rest of her life she remains anxious to know and passes her doubt through Douglas to us.

Having no solution to its central enigma, *The Turn of the Screw* refuses to be read, provides no internal means of knowing when we have finished. Once we have absorbed this dilemma, our reading can continue unconsciously even when the text is in the garbage and we are in our showers. Neither of the two main ways of responding to it is satisfactory. The evidence for each undercuts the evidence favoring the other.

This ambiguity is uncomfortable, perhaps to the point of being terrifying. It is usually disturbing to desire certainty that cannot be had. The discomfort is greater if the issues are made to seem important: the sanity of the governess, the fate of a child's soul, whether there has been a murder. To explain the deeper and more formidable causes of terror in this tale, we need to resurrect the implied reader.

The implied reader is a version of myself I create in response to the elements of the tale as I gradually take in pieces of information and attempt to imagine wholes into which they fit. Upon first reading *The Turn of the Screw,* we are likely to create an implied reader appropriate to a popular horror thriller, an *amusette.* This reader tends to accept the governess's account uncritically. But when Miles dies and she asserts he is saved, we begin the reconstruction of the implied reader, for we have been trapped. We should have paid more attention to the governess as a character. We imagine a new whole in which the governess may or may not be responsible for Miles's death and in which all facts and interpretations become questionable. We find out they are, indeed, questionable, but we also learn that we cannot construct a reading of the governess that has any greater authority than her reading of herself. This leaves us with two implied readers. We are split between one reader who condemns the governess as mistaken and irresponsible and another reader who sees her as brilliant and heroic.

Unable to choose which of these readers to authorize, we are trapped in a dilemma precisely parallel to the governess's. She wants to read the children, but discovers two readings. She never has adequate information to choose between these readings. Because she loves the children, her problem is most intense. She cannot bear to think of hurting them, yet an incorrect choice must positively harm them. In this way she is different from us. She must act, and so she must choose, at the risk of harming those she loves. We cannot literally hurt the governess, and, theoretically at least, we can continue not choosing how to read her for as long as we can bear it.

Our desire for integrity in the construction of an implied reader requires that we remain true to our conceptions and attachments. We cannot deny the power of either reading of the governess without depriving her of her own integrity. As Felman argues, to condemn the governess as a madwoman is to do to her exactly what we would then be accusing her of doing to the children.[22] To condemn her is to condemn ourselves; to absolve her is to deny her request for a true mirroring.

Responding to this tale as it requires becomes increasingly terrifying for the reader. We expect fictions to produce endings for themselves. We enter into the game of creating an implied reader in the faith that the role will close itself. James has created a fiction in which the role closes in on us. The implied reader splits into a vibration between two roles, a vibration that cannot end by itself as long as the reader continues to contemplate the work. Clearly the only ordinary means of escaping this entrapment is to actively forget the experience. This, however, is not very satisfying. Good readers often feel something is unfinished and find themselves returning to read and think again. The more we struggle with this split, the more we feel ourselves under the control of an external force. One way of putting it is that we feel the work controlling us.

We usually begin reading with a willing surrender of control, trusting the story to lift us out of ourselves to a more concentrated and significant level of experience than normal living provides. For many reasons we take pleasure in becoming another self at least slightly different from the self that does the laundry, attends committee meetings, and writes reports. James violates this trust. By splitting the implied reader into incompatible roles, he takes control of the real reader, the one who creates the implied reader, and forces the endless repetition of the tale in its various versions. The real reader is left at the end to find his or her own way—if there is one—of ceasing to vibrate between the split implied reader. If there is no way, the real reader is threatened with permanent transformation into this split implied reader, in perpetual colloquy about the governess and the children.

By violating the reader's expectation of a normal reading game, James makes the tale into an alien force that poses serious psychological danger. Expecting a work of art, I encounter a fictional mad scientist intent upon altering my personality. The work holds my mental being in its claws and tinkers with my sense of who I am. I know I can run screaming from this dark laboratory, but that only postpones what I really must do. I must find a way of regaining control over the situation, a way of closing the work myself.

The means of escape from James's trap is fairly easy to accomplish and to understand, though for most readers, judging from my personal experience as a reader and teacher, it is difficult to discover. The trap is made to hold us. But, by describing it, we have moved toward escaping it. To see how one is entangled is to begin to make possible the loosening of knots. This happens because we have found a perspective not directly available in the text.

We have been doing more than simply rereading the text. We have also constructed the "implied rereader" as a double, entrapped, implied reader. The implied reader is a concept, a name we have given to a dynamic element we can point to and describe in the experience of reading fiction. It is important to notice that we are describing processes of which we are normally unconscious. Only rather an odd reader would maintain an awareness of the implied reader. Instead, normal readers simply become that reader, because it is a necessary part of the reading process. By trying to articulate a particular implied reader, we have been observing ourselves as we read. In this way we mirror the governess's attempt to capture herself in her writing.

But also—and this is quite important—in attempting to read ourselves as we read, we have been following instructions implicit in James's text. On multiple levels James has been calling attention to the fictionality of the self. The governess invents selves for the ghosts and the children, eventually arriving at two versions for the children, and choosing one. She also presents different versions of her own self. Such multiple constructions of the self on the narrative level are repeated on the level of our self-creating activity, the making of implied readers. We make at least two and probably more implied readers.

James encourages awareness of the process of self-creation. He implies in the governess's activities that creating real selves is essentially similar to creating selves in reading fiction. By means of interacting with the symbol systems (culture / novella) into which we enter (birth / reading), we unconsciously build ideas of who we are. James shows this process in the narrative, and he catches us up in its limitations and terrors in the way he organizes the tale. Calling attention to the fictionality of the self hints at how one can successfully "escape" James's trap.

The Turn of the Screw offers perspective after perspective on the characters and events, yet none proves authoritative. This implies there is no authoritative perspective. The events at Bly cannot be read. If there is no master perspective, there is no master self that can see all. If there is no master self, then all selves are exposed as fictional. There is no model of the self to which we should all aspire. Rather, each self is its own fictional construct, belonging to its creator, the invisible awareness at the center of each of us.

This is an intellectual statement of what the reader who locates the main escape route from *The Turn of the Screw* discovers. This enlightenment happens when real readers find they can retreat to their own unique perspectives.

We think of ourselves as the self we are trying to be. But there is another entity that does this thinking, who participates in creating the idea of the self. Contemporary psychoanalysis sometimes calls this entity the subject. We can, for example, speak of the governess as trying to view herself as subject by means of the children. The occupation of the subject is normally to conform to its idea of itself. When reading fiction, however, it is freed temporarily from this work and allowed to play at creating selves.

James captures the self-creating activity of the subject, not allowing it simply to return to self-maintenance, but riveting its attention on the dilemma of the split implied reader. To flee from this dilemma accomplishes the return to normal activity, but with the permanent disturbance of those feuding selves pushed into the background.

The more satisfying solution is to occupy freely the position of subject, to move not back to the activity of maintaining my own self, but rather to the contemplation of the selves among which I can choose, the two before me being the split implied reader and my normal, familiar self. This is a revolutionary step, for it places the real reader in a psychological position that human beings occupy only in their highest moments of contemplation.

In normal life the process of self-creation is largely unconscious and unchosen. Culture lays out paths and often determines rather precisely which a person will follow. Only rarely, often in moments of resistance, does one discover that one has freedom to make oneself. For example, the governess undergoes a revolution of this sort when she accepts that being amused is a good thing and begins to learn how to be amused. Her education and her fate as a governess do not normally offer amusement as a legitimate expectation. Her discovery of the capacity and her willingness to nurture it lead her to a greater freedom of self-creation than her culture would usually allow.

In this novella James has made a moment of conscious self-creation necessary to completing the reading. To escape James's trap the reader must occupy a perspective from which all selves are fictional, the normal self as well as the implied reader. From this perspective all selves are chosen roles. To complete the reading I need only realize (but not necessarily articulate) that the role of split implied reader in *The Turn of the Screw* belongs to the book and not to me.

When I become conscious of the implied reader as a fiction born out of my interaction with the tale, then I know my center of awareness as separate from that self and from all selves I as subject might create. When I surrender this self to the work that stimulated it, I am liberated. I become free of the trap and momentarily free of mere, unconscious conformity to my idea of myself.

From this perspective the implied reader becomes a part of the tale. The tale closes in one sense, though not in another. It closes in that I can stop reading it, for now it is contained within my consciousness, and it no longer threatens to overwhelm me. But it remains open in that our questions about the governess, the children, and the ghosts are still unanswered.

We can see how taking a critical stance by observing ourselves as we read helps to uncover this means of reading the unreadable. That critical stance is an attempt to move outside the hunt for perspectives and thereby to see that search as part of the meaning of the tale. The critical attempt mimics what the successful reader can accomplish without necessarily being able to explain what he or she has done.

Norman Holland describes an analogous solution to the face /

vase problem with the optical illusion. It is true that we cannot normally see both faces and vase simultaneously. This happens because we move from general to specific when we encounter a perceptual problem, returning to the details rather than looking for an alternate perspective. Similarly, once *The Turn of the Screw* catches us in the cycle of rereading, we continue to examine the details for a confirmation of one of the competing readings. According to Holland, we can solve the optical illusion by adopting another perspective, by imagining two faces pressed up against the vase. If we construct this new whole of which the conflicting images are parts, then we can see the illusion as a closed whole rather than two mutually exclusive wholes.[23]

The novella, though whole, remains as silent as ever. The governess's unspeakable secret is never spoken with authority. Why Miles died and in what spiritual state remain mysterious. What things he said no one can say. But now each silence is an acknowledged part of the wholenesses of the tale, of the governess, and of Miles, to name the most important. This is possible because James has forced the reader to occupy the perspective from which the self becomes visible as a fictional creation, delicately balanced over and against one's own silence.

TO SEE IT ALL: MEANINGS OF
THE TURN OF THE SCREW

The Turn of the Screw reflects a worldview quite similar to the one Nina Baym attributes to Nathaniel Hawthorne in *The Scarlet Letter: A Reading.* [24] At the center of this view is a problem that arose in the Enlightenment and became increasingly troubling to the Victorians, the absence of an authoritative reading of the cosmos.

In Western civilization for about a millennium, Christianity successfully claimed to have interpreted the cosmos, to know the meaning and purpose of human life. Though there were competing views, these remained in the minority and were strictly controlled politically and militarily. But following the intellectual and political revolutions of the Enlightenment, the authority of Christianity faded. Religious institutions, already divided by intellectual as well as political strife, lost the power to coerce belief. For James as for Hawthorne the meanings human beings found in life were made by people, not revealed by church or scripture. Their power to compel belief depended upon the power of those who believed, not on the authority of a divine source. Their value was in their utility, in their ability to promote material welfare, social harmony, and individual happiness, rather than in their being true by an objective standard.

The decline of the authority of Christianity is reflected directly in the way critics have read the tale. The governess reads herself through a version of Christianity, but early Freudian readings rejected her theological interpretation in favor of a secular, determinist reading.

Part of the governess's problem is that she feels forced to make final judgments about meaning. This proves virtually impossible because her world is split into apparently contradictory parts, into polar or binary oppositions of presence and absence.

Oppositions of Presence and Absence—Set One

Governess	*Uncle*
Ghosts	Hallucinations
Corrupt children	Innocent children
Visionary governess	Mad governess

These are oppositions that become visible to the governess when she sees the invisible. The uncle is absent, but were he present, he would see the surface or what is present: innocent children and a mad governess. The governess is present, but she sees what is absent, the dead. Her privileged glimpses make her aware of the world as including the invisible. She sees her once fairly simple, narrow world double itself. There is a visible surface of great beauty, and there is a shadowy subsurface, filled with secrets only pointed at by troubling manifestations.

She deals with this enlarged vision of her world just as the theology of her culture would suggest; that is, she constructs a more or less Christian religious explanation. The shadow world of which she sees signs is the realm of evil. The children's souls are at stake. Her duty is to "justify" her view and, if it can be justified, to "save" the children. She is victorious because her theology tells her that confession shows the will to choose good.

Psychoanalytic critics tend to adopt the story she attributes to the absent uncle. For them the split she sees in the world is really a split in the governess that shows she is mad. Like her, they impose an ideology upon the polar oppositions in order to resolve them. Her ideology derives from Christian theology; theirs imposes a belief in psychological determinism. Each approach exposes the inadequacy of comprehensive views that attempt to eliminate rather than accept this split in human perception.

Nevertheless, psychoanalysis is the source of the insight that the split the governess discovers in the world is in herself as well, that it is a product of the mind's attempt to grasp itself and the world. A human mind is indefinitely greater than the self it shows to the world, for each mind contains the potential for becoming untold numbers of selves. The major Freudian readings of *The Turn of the Screw* remind us forcefully of the impossibility of the governess's theological attempt at healing her divided vision. Her assertions that she has saved Miles and is whole demonstrate not the discovery of truth, but the will to believe. The revisions of Freud offered by Lacan, among others, reveal that the traditional Freudian readings, such as those by Edmund Wilson and Oscar Cargill, were also products of a will to believe. They willed to believe not in Christian theology, but in psychoanalytic ideology. Neither approach could heal the split the governess discovered.

This healing cannot take place because the split is fundamental. As contemporary theorists of language and psychology have argued, experience divides when we represent it. What we can represent becomes visible; what we cannot or do not represent remains invisible and silent. Our consciousness consists of what we represent ourselves to be; our unconscious consists in part of whatever remains in ourselves that we fail or refuse to represent.

When we escape James's trap, we do not mend our own conscious / unconscious split, nor do we discover language to resolve any of the text's ambiguities. Instead, we temporarily become conscious of occupying the perspective from which the self is represented. In other words, our escape from *The Turn of the Screw* involves momentarily restraining the usually continuous act of self-creation in order to contemplate that act. In doing so I see that although the self I create is a container of my ideas of who I would be, it does not contain me. Rather, I contain it. I am a "subject" and my identity is an object, the distinct, visible objectification or representation that allows me to act purposefully in the world.

Readings of *The Turn of the Screw* reflect intellectual history. Early readings tended to resolve ambiguity in favor of the governess's Christian view. Later readings tended to favor the approach she thinks the absent uncle would take. Our reading attempts to transcend ideology, to seek out the artistic unity of a literary work that acknowledges and preserves its irresolvable ambiguity. This reading affirms the permanence for human consciousness of the division the governess discovers in her world.

Part of the governess's problem in dealing with the division she discovers is her relation to authority. In the absence of certainty the power of interpretations to compel belief derives from the political / social power of the interpreters. In most areas of Victorian life a young woman would accept and conform to male authority in interpreting. The absence of male authority at Bly makes the governess's situation unique. She is required to become the master in the master's absence. The governess's plight as she attempts to be a master illuminates several aspects of the position of women in her society, a subject that concerned James in most of his fiction. He once said, "Half of life is a sealed book to young unmarried ladies."[25] To get at this subject, it may be helpful to present more oppositions of presence and absence.

Oppositions of Presence and Absence—Set Two

Authority	*Conformity*
Conscious	Unconscious
Language	Reality
Figure	Meaning
Male	Female
Master	Servant
Uncle	Governess
Governess	Children

This list can lead in many directions, not all of which are articulated here. We follow it mainly into the exploration of the governess's position as a woman. Doing so reveals meanings related to gender and class roles in the tale.

This list of oppositions could include another label in each column. At the top of the left column we could have put *presence*, at the top of the right *absence*. To the Victorian mind, for social order to be sustained, each entity in the right column was to be subordinated to its opposite in the left, as is indicated by the labels *authority* and *conformity*. This means that in several important senses, those entities on the right were to be silent. The woman, the servant, the governess, the children—these were not to have wills of their own, but to conform to the male will—the master, the uncle, the governess.

In the last two pairs, however, we see an anomaly. In this tale the uncle is absent and the governess present. She has been delegated his authority over Bly. His absence deprives her of what her society routinely supplies its respectable women, the sustaining authority of the male master. The uncle turns over his authority to his opposite, a young, inexperienced female of significantly lower social standing. By doing so, he creates what might be seen as an aberration from Victorian culture, though in fact gentry commonly turned virtually the whole care of their children over to servants.

Because she loves the uncle, the governess's response to his abdication is to become his agent. She behaves as a daughter or wife would be expected to. She willingly subordinates herself to him, but in his absence this proves difficult. She needs his approving look. Her longing to see and be seen is answered by the ghosts. In seeing them, whether or not they are real, she achieves a view of herself that he will not give her. Once she has achieved this view, she feels independent of his authority, which now threatens the authority of her vision of the children and even the children themselves. But when her view prevails, it also fails to be comprehensive. Certainty eludes her; hence her repeating her story to Douglas.

The absence of the uncle displaces the governess from the position she would normally occupy, making her sole rather than subordinate authority at Bly. His absence betrays her legitimate expectations, but it also liberates her to develop and exercise mastery usually held only by males. But in successfully developing and exercising this mastery, she exposes its fictionality, its failure to cover reality.

Her escape from authority releases her vision and shows her the world divided. Her attempt to stitch this rent reveals that she has been seduced. The uncle is not really a master at all. Rather, he has pretended to be master by ordering her to be his agent. He had the power to give that order, but not the control of the situation he implied she would receive by obeying.

In ideologies, such as many forms of Christianity and psychoanalysis, a language claims to contain reality; it asserts the mastery of meaning. Language and the portentous figure have authority in human discourse, but reality and meaning elude them. When the governess finally grasped Miles, he was dead. When she saw it all, it was nothing. When she told the whole story, she evoked silence. The figure or letter is portentous, but the letter itself is the only means by which we can indicate the portent. We cannot touch meaning itself as a way of confirming the reading we have attached to the figure.

In the world James creates no one can achieve certainty. In Victorian society men claimed this power and denied it to women. Victorians worried about maintaining order in a time of fairly rapid change. Their instinctive response to disorder was to repress it.

The uncle shows one way of repressing one's fear of loss of

control over society. If he feels inadequate to raise children, then he assumes it can be done and delegates his authority and responsibility to the governess. A good Victorian girl, she believes in his authority and tries to exercise it on his behalf. This situation reflects the archetypal, middle-class, Victorian household, where the man, dirtied and worn by contact with the vicious world, delegates the moral education of himself and his children to the wife who has been shielded as much as possible from knowledge of that world. The master's inadequacy is thus hidden behind his designation of another in his place. That the other is an innocent sets her up for many possible disasters of which we can read in the history of Victorian marriage. One kind of disaster is acted out by the governess.

In this tale, then, the power to define reality is essentially political. It belongs to people who are able by some means to achieve the authority to compel the acceptance of their interpretations. We see this when we reflect that a man in the governess's position would normally have other resources upon which to draw to bolster his authority, such as friends from the university. He would have no hesitations about dealing with the headmaster. He would occupy a position of authority with more comfort because he would not be intellectually isolated and because his whole life experience would have prepared him to command a certain authority.

The governess, however, is much more tentative than a man would be, isolated from intellectual peers and not used to exercising authority. This makes her especially sensitive to the fictionality of mastery. Because a man could so much more easily establish his authority, he would be less likely to discover the degree to which his confidence in his judgments derives from his political power.

Because she is a woman in a male-dominated society, the governess is "privileged" in the sense that she has access to what her society declares invisible, her own individuality and whatever seeks to be known by putting forth appearances of the supernatural. Observing her dilemma and how she handles it reveals her position as one normally without authority in a time when authority is the source of meaning. She is especially able to point toward aspects of reality that disappear from within the Victorian perspective, thus exposing the illusion that it includes all reality.

EDUCATING THE IMAGINATION

To reread *The Turn of the Screw* as we have done is an education for the imagination. That Western civilization lost a unified, shared religious view of the meaning of the universe did not lead to a unified, shared secular view of that meaning. Not in James's time nor since has there been agreement concerning how individuals and societies should adjust to the relativism implicit in the likelihood that there is no single, absolute perspective on meaning available to humanity. A number of major American writers including James's older contemporaries Herman Melville and Nathaniel Hawthorne and the greatest of the next generation, such as Ernest Hemingway and William Faulkner, have represented the world as without a knowable meaning, and all of these have suggested in varying ways that happiness grows out of creating an admirable self while sustaining the deepest possible communion with others. Implicit in such an idea is an ideal that sheds light from two directions upon how this tale educates the imagination. The ideal is of a community that supports all individuals and of individuals who never sever themselves from that community.

One way this tale communicates this ideal is by criticizing ideology. Ideology means the belief that one's chosen way of organizing reality is absolute and supercedes all others. To complete *The Turn of the Screw* one must at least momentarily act as if one believes that all perspectives are fictional and therefore that any attempt to organize reality must leave silences and omissions. This realization does not preclude organizing reality. In James one has no choice but to impose meanings upon the world, and which meanings one chooses makes a difference. To decide what to do about the apparently endangered children, the governess must authorize an interpretation. Reading this tale encourages us to recognize that our meanings are partial and provisional.

Because her society imposes absolute repressions—do not talk to the master; do not speak of ghosts or sex to the children—the governess is trapped in ideologies. Her society forbids options she needs, confining her to her solo reading. Though she is aware of the partiality of her reading, she must act anyway. When Flora rises the first time in the night, the governess longs to talk frankly with her. She has a similar feeling when she goes to Miles's room on the night after he opens the subject of school. It seems clear that in their last interview Miles wants to speak frankly with her, but he too is hedged about with inhibitions and prohibitions. Only in telling her story does the governess approach her idea of frankness. These traps seem to originate in the totalitarian nature of social ideology. If ideologies tend to insist upon their comprehensiveness in any age, this novella points at their limitations.

By criticizing ideology the tale also implies a kind of etiquette of imposing meaning. The ideals of the individual and society implicit in James's worldview suggest that an individual's insistence upon a meaning is limited by the community's need to sustain love, the primary social bond. Likewise, the community's need to preserve the secondary institutions that support love (for example, marriage, family, and education) is limited by the individual's need to maintain an admirable self.

The tale points to this etiquette when it makes us care for the governess. To care for her involves refusing to force one meaning upon her to the exclusion of other real possibilities. The crisis comes precisely when she is unfairly coerced to impose a meaning upon the children without their voluntary assent. That she is most a victim when she makes the children into possible victims shows the failure of her community both to let her truly be an individual and to recognize the limits of its own ideology.

At the center of this complex of meanings is the failure to love. We create ourselves out of the images of the lovable our society offers us. We seem to want those images to be uniquely our own and yet to be loved by those close to us. We make ourselves for communion. And community seems to be that sense of wholeness we share with those who were the sources and become the reflections of those lovable images.

When Western culture lost the grand unity of the Christian world-view, it gradually reformed into the present uneasy pluralism of multiple competing ideologies. Often ferocious and bloody, this competition fosters authoritarian thought. Western European and American societies have tended to resist the dominance of a single ideology, but the resulting pluralism intensifies the tension in normal people who frequently long for certainty about life's meaning. We observe daily the invective of communities of belief attempting to assert their unique possession of the Truth. Such behavior demonstrates a failure to love, to consider the perspective of the stranger as valid.

The governess fails to love the children, for she never successfully discovers or constructs their perspective. Yet she, like the children, seems uniquely formed for loving, for her powers of constructing the perspectives of others are formidable. Her community fails to love her, for it excludes her perspective and condemns her to function in comparative silence and isolation. If we judge her reading as either correct or incorrect, we fail to love her by excluding part of her perspective. These failures are all unconscious and unintentional. Her rationale for her choices is that she loves the children. Her society's rationale for "protecting" her would be stated in terms of its special care for women. Our choice of one of her readings would be justified by our care either for her or for the children. Each failure stems not from deliberate choices to be criminal, but from the limitations of the perspectives we adopt. Without an appreciation of the limits of our perspectives, we cannot discover the proper etiquette, and we cannot love or be loved successfully.

The Turn of the Screw educates the imagination for a moral life in a world where meanings are provisional and limited. By leading the reader into rereading, this story provides more than the usual practice in the construction of others' perspectives. By forcing the reader to take the perspective from which the self and all possible selves are fictional, this tale stimulates an awareness of meanings as constructs rather than givens. By placing the reader in the position of judging the governess as a loved one, the novella points to the limits of constructed meanings and to the etiquette of dealing with the constructions of others. By showing ideology to be one cause of failures to love, this work challenges us to subordinate the imposition of meaning to the ultimate goal of loving communion.

Notes

1. Nina Baym, *"The Scarlet Letter": A Reading* (Boston: Twayne, 1986), xviii–xx.

2. Edna Kenton, "Henry James to the Ruminant Reader: *The Turn of the Screw*," in *A Casebook on Henry James's "The Turn of the Screw*," ed. Gerald Willen (New York: Crowell, 1960), 102–14.

3. Edmund Wilson, "The Ambiguity of Henry James," in *A Casebook*, 115–53.

4. Tzvetan Todorov, *The Fantastic*, trans. Richard Howard (Ithaca, N.Y.: Cornell University Press, 1973), 43.

5. Ibid., 43.

6. Wolfgang Iser, *The Act of Reading* (Baltimore: Johns Hopkins University Press, 1978), 35–36.

7. Shoshana Felman, "Turning the Screw of Interpretation," in *Literature and Psychoanalysis*, ed. Shoshana Felman (Baltimore: Johns Hopkins University Press, 1982), 138–40.

8. Leon Edel, *Henry James: A Life* (New York: Harper & Row, 1985), 392.

9. Ibid., 446–47.

10. Christine Brooke-Rose, *A Rhetoric of the Unreal* (Cambridge and London: Cambridge University Press, 1981), 158–88.

11. Ibid., 175–87.

12. Ibid., 181.

13. Peter G. Beidler, "The Governess and the Ghosts," *PMLA* 100, no. 1 (1985):96–97.

14. E. A. Sheppard, *Henry James and "The Turn of the Screw"* (London: Aukland University Press and Oxford University Press, 1974), 208–11.

15. Brooke-Rose, *Rhetoric of the Unreal*, 172–76.

16. Ibid., 177–78.

17. Eli Siegel, *James and the Children* (New York: Definition Press, 1968), 38.

18. For a more detailed presentation of this material, see Ellie Ragland-Sullivan, *Jacques Lacan and the Philosophy of Psychoanalysis* (Urbana: University of Illinois Press, 1986), 1–67, and Stuart Schneiderman, "Lacan's Early Contribution to Psychoanalysis," in *Returning to Freud: Clinical Psychoanalysis in the School of Lacan*, ed. Stuart Schneiderman (New Haven, Conn.: Yale University Press, 1980), 1–8.

19. Shlomith Rimmon, *The Concept of Ambiguity: The Example of Henry James* (Chicago: University of Chicago Press, 1977), 137.

20. Henry James, "The Pupil," in *Tales of Henry James,* ed. Christof Wegelin (New York: Norton, 1984), 207.

21. Terry Heller, *The Delights of Terror* (Urbana: University of Illinois Press, 1987), 170.

22. Felman, "Turning the Screw," esp. 190.

23. Norman Holland, *The I* (New Haven, Conn.: Yale University Press, 1985), 124.

24. Baym, "*The Scarlet Letter,*" esp. chaps. 4 and 5.

25. James E. Miller, *Theory of Fiction: Henry James* (Lincoln: University of Nebraska Press, 1972), 135.

Selected Bibliography

Primary Sources

Editions

The Novels and Tales of Henry James. Rev. ed., with prefaces by James. New York: Scribners, 1907–17. This twenty-six-volume collection, known as the New York Edition, provides the authoritative texts of the pieces James selected to represent his life's work. Macmillan of London reprinted this edition under the same title, but with additions of works James had excluded, bringing it to thirty-five volumes, 1921–23. Many useful paperback editions and selections are available. Those of special interest to readers of this book are listed below.

Edel, Leon, editor. *Henry James: Stories of the Supernatural.* New York: Taplinger, 1970.

Kimbrough, Robert, editor. *Henry James: The Turn of the Screw.* Norton Critical Edition. New York: Norton, 1966. This edition contains most of James's commentary on the novella as well as a number of the important critical essays.

Wegelin, Christof, editor. *Tales of Henry James.* New York: Norton, 1984.

Fiction

Roderick Hudson. Boston: Osgood, 1876; London: Macmillan, 1879.

The American. Boston: Osgood, 1877; London: Ward, Lock, 1877.

The Europeans: A Sketch. London: Macmillan, 1878; Boston: Houghton, Osgood, 1879.

Daisy Miller: A Study. New York: Harper, 1878.

Washington Square. New York: Harper, 1881.

The Portrait of a Lady. London: Macmillan, 1881; Boston and New York: Houghton Mifflin, 1882.

The Bostonians. London and New York: Macmillan, 1886.

The Princess Casamassima. London and New York: Macmillan, 1886.

The Lesson of the Master. New York and London: Macmillan, 1892.

The Spoils of Poynton. London: Heinemann, 1897; Boston and New York: Houghton Mifflin, 1897.

What Maisie Knew. London: Heinemann, 1897; Chicago and New York: Stone, 1897.

In the Cage. London: Duckworth, 1898; Chicago and New York: Stone, 1898.

The Two Magics: The Turn of the Screw, Covering End. London: Heinemann, 1898; New York and London: Macmillan, 1898.

The Awkward Age. London: Heinemann, 1899; New York and London: Harper, 1899.

The Sacred Fount. New York: Scribners, 1901; London: Methuen, 1901.

The Wings of the Dove. New York: Scribners, 1902; Westminster: Constable, 1902.

The Ambassadors. London: Methuen, 1903; New York and London: Harper, 1903.

The Golden Bowl. New York: Scribners, 1904; London: Methuen, 1905.

The Complete Tales of Henry James. Edited by Leon Edel. Philadelphia: Lippincott, 1962–65.

Other Writing

Hawthorne. London: Macmillan, 1879; New York: Harper, 1880.

Theory of Fiction: Henry James. Edited by James E. Miller, Jr. Lincoln: University of Nebraska Press, 1972.

The Notebooks of Henry James. Edited by F. O. Matthiessen and Kenneth M. Murdock. New York: Oxford University Press, 1947.

The Complete Plays of Henry James. Edited by Leon Edel. Philadelphia: Lippincott, 1949.

The Future of the Novel: Essays on the Art of Fiction. Edited by Leon Edel. New York: Vintage, 1956.

Henry James: Letters. Edited by Leon Edel. Cambridge: Harvard University Press: Belknap Press, 1974–84.

Secondary Sources

Biographies

Beach, Joseph Warren. *The Method of Henry James*. Rev. ed. Philadelphia: Saifer, 1954.

Dupee, Frederick W. *Henry James*. New York: Sloane, 1951.

———, editor. *Henry James: Autobiography*. New York: Criterion, 1956.

Edel, Leon. *Henry James: A Life*. New York: Harper & Row, 1985.

McElderry, Bruce R., Jr. *Henry James*. New York: Twayne, 1965.

Powers, Lyall H. *Henry James: An Introduction and Interpretation*. New York: Holt, Rinehart, & Winston, 1967.

Critical Studies: Books on James

Banta, Martha. *Henry James and the Occult*. Bloomington: Indiana University Press, 1972. Considers *The Turn of the Screw* in relation to James's use of the supernatural in his fiction.

Brooke-Rose, Christine. *A Rhetoric of the Unreal*. Cambridge and London: Cambridge University Press, 1981.Chapters 5 to 8 present detailed analyses of style and narrative voice in *The Turn of the Screw*.

Brooks, Van Wyck. *The Pilgrimage of Henry James*. New York: Dutton. 1925. Discusses James's alienation from America.

Cranfill, Thomas Mabry, and Robert Lanier Clark, Jr. *An Anatomy of "The Turn of the Screw."* New York: Gordian Press, 1971.Though often self-contradictory and ultimately incoherent, this is a rich source of ways the governess's authority may be undercut by clever readers.

Krook, Dorothea. *The Ordeal of Consciousness in Henry James*. Cambridge and London: Cambridge University Press, 1962. An excellent study of James's works, with a thoughtful reading of *The Turn of the Screw*.

Pelham, Edgar. *Henry James: Man and Author*. Boston: Houghton Mifflin, 1927. Argues that James gained an objective view of America by residing in Europe.

Rimmon, Shlomith. *The Concept of Ambiguity: The Example of Henry James*. Chicago: University of Chicago Press, 1977. Places *The Turn of the Screw* in the context of James's development of techniques of ambiguity. Especially helpful for explanations of the techniques.

Rowe, John Carlos. *The Theoretical Dimensions of Henry James*. Madison: University of Wisconsin Press, 1984. Includes a Lacanian study of the significance of the absence of authority from *The Turn of the Screw*.

Sheppard, E. A. *Henry James and "The Turn of the Screw."* London: Aukland University Press and Oxford University Press, 1974. A thorough exploration of James's intellectual and artistic sources for *The Turn of the Screw.*

Siegel, Eli. *James and the Children.* New York: Definition Press, 1968. A quirky but insightful discussion of possible evil in Miles and Flora.

Willen, Gerald, editor. *A Casebook on Henry James's "The Turn of the Screw."* New York: Crowell, 1960. Contains several of the more important critical essays, including those by Edna Kenton, Edmund Wilson, Robert Heilman, and Harold C. Goddard.

Critical Studies: Articles and Book Chapters on James

Beidler, Peter G. "The Governess and the Ghosts." *PMLA* 100, no.1 (1985):96–97. Presents W. H. Myers's letter interpreting the relationship between the ghosts and the children as sexually perverse on several levels.

Booth, Wayne C. "Indifference to the Writer's Task: Telling a Ghost Story." In *Critical Understanding,* 284–301. Chicago: University of Chicago Press, 1979. Perhaps the most persuasive argument that James intended the ghosts to be taken as real.

Boren, Lynda S. "The Performing Self: Psychodrama in Austen, James, and Woolf." *Centennial Review* 30 (1986):1–24. Looks at the governess as a woman aspiring to the freedom to create herself, comparing her to characters in Jane Austen and Virginia Woolf.

Cohen, Paula Marantz. "Freud's *Dora* and James's *Turn of the Screw*: Two Treatments of the Female 'Case.'" *Criticism* 28 (1986):73–87. Argues that James succeeds in allowing the feminine a voice in the governess, while Freud represses the voice of Dora.

Crowl, Susan. "Aesthetic Allegory in *The Turn of the Screw.*" *Novel* 4 (1971):107–22. Shows how the unfinished form of the story reflects the incompleteness of the governess's reading of the children.

Eaton, Marcia. "James's Turn of the Speech-Act." *British Journal of Aesthetics* 23, no. 4 (1983):331–45. Notes features that suggest the governess's narrative is an excuse or explanation.

Felman, Shoshana. "Turning the Screw of Interpretation." In *Literature and Psychoanalysis,* edited by Shoshana Felman, 94–207. Baltimore: Johns Hopkins University Press, 1982. Uses Lacanian psychoanalysis to probe the tale's unreadability and its struggling readers.

Heller, Terry. "The Master's Trap: James's *The Turn of the Screw.*" In *The Delights of Terror,* 147–68. Urbana: University of Illinois Press, 1987. Examines the story in relation to genres of the tale of terror.

Selected Bibliography

Kauffman, Linda S. "The Author of our Woe: Virtue Recorded in *The Turn of the Screw.*" *Nineteenth Century Fiction* 36 (1981):176–92. Argues that the frame narrator is probably a woman.

Krook, Dorothea. "The Madness of Art: Further Reflections on the Ambiguity of Henry James." *Hebrew University Studies in Literature* 1 (1972):25–38. Argues that James's ambiguity in this tale is complete, deliberate, and meaningful.

Mansell, Darrell. "The Ghosts of Language in *The Turn of the Screw.*" *Modern Language Quarterly* 46 (1985):48–63. Analyzes the style of the story to show how it creates significant silences.

Miall, David S. "Designed Horror: James's Vision of Evil in *The Turn of the Screw.*" *Nineteenth Century Fiction* 39 (1984):305–27. Examines relationships between the story and a major contemporary ghostly manifestation investigated by the Society for Psychical Research.

Murphy, Kevin. "The Unfixable Text: Bewilderment of Vision in *The Turn of the Screw.*" *Texas Studies in Literature and Language* 20 (1978):538–51. Explores analogies between the reader and the governess.

Nardin, Jane. "*The Turn of the Screw*: The Victorian Background." *Mosaic* 12 (1978):131–42. Studies the effects on the governess of Victorian class and sexual morality.

Schrero, Elliot M. "Exposure in *The Turn of the Screw.*" *Modern Philology* 78 (1981):261–74. Explores probable Victorian reactions to *The Turn of the Screw* based on attitudes toward governesses, schools, servants, and orphans.

Voeglin, Eric. "*The Turn of the Screw.*" *Southern Review* 7 (1971):3–48. Places the tale in a context of Western intellectual history.

Interpretive Theories and Backgrounds: Books and Articles

Day, William Patrick. *In the Circles of Fear and Desire: A Study of Gothic Fantasy.* Chicago: University of Chicago Press, 1985.

Freud, Sigmund. *On Creativity and the Unconscious.* Edited by Benjamin Nelson. New York: Harper & Row, 1958.

Gallop, Jane. *The Daughter's Seduction: Feminism and Psychoanalysis.* Ithaca, N.Y.: Cornell University Press, 1982.

———. *Reading Lacan.* Ithaca, N.Y.: Cornell University Press, 1985.

Holland, Norman. *The I.* New Haven, Conn.: Yale University Press, 1985.

Houghton, Walter E. *The Victorian Frame of Mind.* New Haven, Conn.: Yale University Press, 1957.

Hume, Kathryn. *Fantasy and Mimeses.* New York: Methuen, 1984.

Iser, Wolfgang. *The Act of Reading*. Baltimore: Johns Hopkins University Press, 1978.

———. *The Implied Reader*. Baltimore: Johns Hopkins University Press, 1974.

Jackson, Rosemary. *Fantasy*. New York: Methuen, 1981.

Jameson, Fredric. "Imaginary and Symbolic in Lacan: Marxism, Psychoanalytic Criticism, and the Problems of the Subject." In *Literature and Psychoanalysis*, edited by Shoshana Felman, 338–95. Baltimore: Johns Hopkins University Press, 1982.

Liddell, Robert. *A Treatise on the Novel*. London: Jonathan Cape, 1947.

Punter, David. *The Literature of Terror*. New York: Longman, 1980.

Ragland-Sullivan, Ellie. *Jacques Lacan and the Philosophy of Psychoanalysis*. Urbana: University of Illinois Press, 1986.

Schneiderman, Stuart. "Lacan's Early Contributions to Psychoanalysis." In *Returning to Freud: Clinical Psychoanalysis in the School of Lacan*, edited by Stuart Schneiderman, 1–8. New Haven, Conn.: Yale University Press, 1980.

———. "The Other Lacan." In *Returning to Freud: Clinical Psychoanalysis in the School of Lacan*, edited by Stuart Schneiderman, 9–16. New Haven, Conn.: Yale University Press, 1980.

Siebers, Tobin. *The Romantic Fantastic*. Ithaca, N.Y.: Cornell University Press, 1984.

Smith, Joseph H., and William Kerrigan, editors. *Interpreting Lacan*. New Haven, Conn.: Yale University Press, 1983.

Tompkins, Jane P., editor. *Reader-Response Criticism*. Baltimore: Johns Hopkins University Press, 1980.

Thompson, G. Richard, editor. *The Gothic Imagination*. Pullman: Washington State University Press, 1974.

Todorov, Tzvetan. *The Fantastic: A Structural Approach to a Literary Genre*. Translated by Richard Howard. Ithaca, N.Y.: Cornell University Press, 1973.

Index

Index

About the Author

Terry Heller is professor of English at Coe College, Cedar Rapids, Iowa. He is the author of *The Delights of Terror* and of articles and reviews that have appeared in *Arizona Quarterly, Gothic, Thalia, Dictionary of Literary Biography,* and *The Annual Review of Fantasy and Science Fiction.*